101 Granny Squares™

General Information

Many of the products used in this pattern book can be purchased from local craft, fabric and variety stores, or from the Annie's Attic Needlecraft Catalog (see Customer Service information on page 83).

Square 1

FINISHED SIZE
7 inches from point to point

GAUGE
Rnds 1 & 2 = 3 inches

PATTERN NOTES
Join with slip stitch as indicated unless otherwise stated.

Square is made with 1 color of medium (worsted) weight yarn.

SPECIAL STITCHES
Beginning cluster (beg cl): Ch 3 (*counts as first dc*), holding back last lp of each st on hook, 3 dc in place indicated, yo, pull through all lps on hook.

Cluster (cl): Holding back last lp of each st on hook, 4 dc in place indicated, yo, pull through all lps on hook.

INSTRUCTIONS
SQUARE
Rnd 1: With size H hook, ch 4, sl st in first ch to form ring, ch 4 (*counts as first dc and ch-1*), [dc in ring, ch 1] 11 times, **join** (*see Pattern Notes*) in 3rd ch of beg ch-4. (*12 dc, 12 ch sps*)

Rnd 2: Sl st in first ch sp, **beg cl** (*see Special Stitches*) in same ch sp, *ch 2, **cl** (*see Special Stitches*) in next ch sp, ch 3, tr in next st, ch 3, cl in next ch sp, ch 2**, cl in next ch sp, rep from * around, ending last rep at **, join in beg cl. (*4 tr, 12 cls*)

Rnd 3: Ch 1, sc in beg cl, *ch 3, sk in next cl, 4 dc in next ch-3 sp, ch 2, (tr, ch 3, sl st in top of last tr) in next st, ch 2, 4 dc in next ch-3 sp, ch 3**, sk next cl, sc in next cl, rep from * around, ending last rep at **, join in beg sc. Fasten off. ∎

Square 2

FINISHED SIZE
5 inches square

GAUGE
Rnds 1 & 2 = 3½ inches

PATTERN NOTES
Join with slip stitch as indicated unless otherwise stated.

Square is made with 2 colors of medium (worsted) weight yarn.

SPECIAL STITCHES
Beginning cluster (beg cl): Ch 2 *(counts as first hdc)*, holding back last lp of each st on hook, 3 hdc in place indicated, yo, pull through all lps on hook.

Cluster (cl): Holding back last lp of each st on hook, 4 hdc in place indicated, yo, pull through all lps on hook.

INSTRUCTIONS
SQUARE
Rnd 1: With size H hook, ch 5, sl st in first ch to form ring, ch 5 *(counts as first dc and ch-2)*, [dc in ring, ch 2] 7 times, **join** *(see Pattern Notes)* in 3rd ch of beg ch-5. *(8 dc, 8 ch sps)*

Rnd 2: Sl st in first ch sp, **beg cl** *(see Special Stitches)* in same ch sp, ch 5, [**cl** *(see Special Stitches)* in next ch sp, ch 5] around, join in beg cl. Fasten off.

Rnd 3: Join next color with sc in first st, *ch 2, working over ch-5 on last rnd, dc in next st on rnd 1, ch 2**, sc in next cl, rep from * around, ending last rep at **, join in beg sc.

Rnd 4: Sl st in first ch sp, ch 1, sc in same ch sp, ch 3, [sc in next ch sp, ch 3] around, join in beg sc.

Rnd 5: Sl st in first ch sp, ch 3 *(counts as first dc)*, (dc, ch 2, 2 dc) in same ch sp *(corner)*, *ch 2, sc in next ch sp, [ch 3, sc in next ch sp] twice, ch 2**, (2 dc, ch 2, 2 dc) in next ch sp *(corner)*, rep from * around, ending last rep at **, join in 3rd ch of beg ch-3. Fasten off. ■

Square 3

GAUGE
Rnds 1 & 2 = 3½ inches

PATTERN NOTES
Join with slip stitch as indicated unless otherwise stated.

Square is made with 3 colors of medium (worsted) weight yarn.

SPECIAL STITCHES

Beginning cluster (beg cl): Ch 3 *(counts as first dc)*, holding back last lp of each st on hook, 2 dc in place indicated, yo, pull through all lps on hook.

Cluster (cl): Holding back last lp of each st on hook, 3 dc in place indicated, yo, pull through all lps on hook.

INSTRUCTIONS
SQUARE

Rnd 1: With size H hook, ch 4, sl st in first ch to form ring, ch 4 *(counts as first dc and ch-1)*, [dc in ring, ch 1] 11 times, **join** *(see Pattern Notes)* in 3rd ch of beg ch-4. Fasten off. *(12 dc, 12 ch sps)*

Rnd 2: Join next color with sl st in any ch sp, **beg cl** *(see Special Stitches)* in same ch sp, ch 3, [**cl** *(see Special Stitches)* in next ch sp, ch 3] around, join in beg cl. Fasten off.

Rnd 3: Join next color with sc in any ch sp, ch 5, [sc in next ch sp, ch 5] around, join in beg sc. Fasten off.

Rnd 4: Join first color with sl st in any ch sp, ch 3 *(counts as first dc)*, (4 dc, ch 3, 5 dc) in same ch sp *(corner)*, *ch 1, sc in next ch sp, ch 5, sc in next ch sp, ch 1**, (5 dc, ch 3, 5 dc) in next ch sp *(corner)*, rep from * around, ending last rep at **, join in beg sc. Fasten off. ■

Square 4

FINISHED SIZE
6 inches square

GAUGE
Rnds 1–3 = 3 inches

PATTERN NOTES
Join with slip stitch as indicated unless otherwise stated.

Square is made with 3 colors of medium (worsted) weight yarn.

INSTRUCTIONS
SQUARE

Rnd 1: With size H hook, ch 6, sl st in first ch to form ring, ch 1, 16 sc in ring, **join** *(see Pattern Notes)* in beg sc.

Rnd 2: Ch 1, sc in first st, *ch 10, sk next 3 sts**, sc in next st, rep from * around, ending last rep at **, join in beg sc.

Rnd 3: Ch 1, sc in first st, *11 sc in next ch sp**, sc in next st, rep from * around, ending last rep at **, join in beg sc. Fasten off.

Rnd 4: Join next color with sc in center st of any 11-sc group, ch 3, sc in same st *(corner)*, *sc in each of next 11 sts**, (sc, ch 3, sc) in next st *(corner)*, rep from * around, ending last rep at **, join in beg sc. Fasten off.

Rnd 5: Join next color with sc in any corner ch sp, ch 3, sc in same ch sp, *sc in each st across to next corner ch sp**, (sc, ch 3, sc) in corner ch sp, rep from * around, ending last rep at **, join in beg sc. Fasten off.

Rnd 6: Join 2nd color with sc in any corner ch sp, ch 3, sc in same ch sp, *sc in each st across to next corner ch sp**, (sc, ch 3, sc) in corner ch sp, rep from * around, ending last rep at **, join in beg sc. Fasten off.

Rnd 7: Join 3rd color with sc in any corner ch sp, ch 3, sc in same ch sp, *sc in each st across to next corner ch sp**, (sc, ch 3, sc) in corner ch sp, rep from * around, ending last rep at **, join in beg sc. Fasten off.

Rnd 8: Join first color with sc in any corner ch sp, ch 3, sc in same ch sp, *sc in each st across to next corner ch sp**, (sc, ch 3, sc) in corner ch sp, rep from * around, ending last rep at **, join in beg sc. Fasten off. ∎

Square 5

FINISHED SIZE
7½ inches square

GAUGE
Rnds 1 & 2 = 3 inches

PATTERN NOTES
Chain-3 at beginning of row or round counts as first double crochet unless otherwise stated.

Join with slip stitch as indicated unless otherwise stated.

Square is made with 1 color of medium (worsted) weight yarn.

SPECIAL STITCH
Popcorn (pc): 5 dc in place indicated, drop lp from hook, insert hook in first dc of group, pull dropped lp through, ch 1 to secure.

INSTRUCTIONS
SQUARE
Rnd 1: With size H hook, ch 6, sl st in first ch to form ring, **ch 3** (see Pattern Notes), dc in ring, *pc (see Special Stitch) in ring**, 4 dc in ring, rep from * 4 times, ending last rep at **, 2 dc in ring, **join** (see Pattern Notes) in 3rd ch of beg ch-3. (4 pc, 16 dc)

Rnd 2: Ch 3, dc in same st, *dc in each of next 3 sts, 2 dc in next st, ch 1**, 2 dc in next st, rep from * around, ending last rep at **, join in 3rd ch of beg ch-3. (28 dc, 4 ch sps)

Rnd 3: Ch 3, dc in same st, *dc in next st, pc in next st, dc in next st, pc in next st, dc in next st, 2 dc in next st, ch 2**, 2 dc in next st, rep from * around, ending last rep at **, join in 3rd ch of beg ch-3. (8 pc, 28 dc)

Rnd 4: Ch 3, dc in same st, *dc in each of next 7 sts, 2 dc in next st, ch 3**, 2 dc in next st, rep from * around, ending last rep at **, join in 3rd ch of beg ch-3. (44 dc)

Rnd 5: Ch 3, dc in same st, *dc in each of next 2 sts, [pc in next st, dc in next st] 3 times, dc in next st, 2 dc in next st, ch 4**, 2 dc in next st, rep from * around, ending last rep at **, join in 3rd ch of beg ch-3. (12 pc, 40 dc)

Rnd 6: Ch 3, dc in same st, *dc in each of next 11 sts, 2 dc in next st, ch 5**, 2 dc in next st, rep from * around, ending last rep at **, join in 3rd ch of beg ch-3. Fasten off. ∎

Square 6

FINISHED SIZE
5 inches square

GAUGE
Rnds 1 & 2 = 4 inches

PATTERN NOTES
Join with slip stitch as indicated unless otherwise stated.

Square is made with 3 colors of medium (worsted) weight yarn.

SPECIAL STITCH
Puff stitch (puff st): [Yo, insert hook in place indicated, yo, pull lp through] 3 times, yo, pull through all lps on hook.

INSTRUCTIONS
SQUARE
Rnd 1: With size H hook, ch 5, sl st in first ch to form ring, ch 5 (*counts as first tr and ch-1*), [tr in ring, ch 1] 11 times, **join** (*see Pattern Notes*) in 4th ch of beg ch-5. Fasten off.

Rnd 2: Join next color with sl st in any ch sp, **puff st** (*see Special Stitch*) in same ch sp, ch 1, puff st in same ch sp, ch 1, (puff st, ch 1) twice in each ch sp around, join in first puff st. Fasten off.

Rnd 3: Join next color with sl st in any ch sp, ch 6 (*counts as first tr and ch-2*), tr in same ch sp, *ch 1, dc in next ch sp, [ch 1, hdc in next ch sp] 3 times, ch 1, dc in next ch sp, ch 1**, (tr, ch 2, tr) in next ch sp, rep from * around, ending last rep at **, join in 4th ch of beg ch-6.

Rnd 4: Sl st in first ch sp, ch 1, (sc, ch 3, sc) in same ch sp, *[ch 1, sc in next ch sp] 6 times, ch 1**, (sc, ch 3, sc) in next ch sp, rep from * around, ending last rep at **, join in beg sc. Fasten off. ∎

Square 7

FINISHED SIZE
4¼ inches square

GAUGE
Rnds 1 & 2 = 2¼ inches

PATTERN NOTES
Join with slip stitch as indicated unless otherwise stated.

Square is made with 4 colors of medium (worsted) weight yarn.

INSTRUCTIONS
SQUARE

Rnd 1: With size H hook, ch 4, sl st in first ch to form ring, ch 3 *(counts as first dc)*, 15 dc in ring, **join** *(see Pattern Notes)* in 3rd ch of beg ch-3. Fasten off. *(16 dc)*

Rnd 2: Join next color with sc in any st, *sk next st, 5 hdc in next st, sk next st**, sc in next st, rep from * around, ending last rep at **, join in beg sc. Fasten off.

Rnd 3: Join next color with sc in center hdc of any hdc group, *7 dc in next sc**, sc in center hdc of next hdc group, rep from * around, ending last rep at **, join in beg sc. Fasten off.

Rnd 4: Join next color with sc in center dc of any dc group, *9 tr in next sc**, sc in center dc of next dc group, rep from * around, ending last rep at **, join in beg sc. Fasten off. ■

Square 8

FINISHED SIZE
6 inches square

GAUGE
Rnds 1 & 2 = 3¾ inches

PATTERN NOTES
Join with slip stitch as indicated unless otherwise stated.

Square is made with 1 color of medium (worsted) weight yarn.

INSTRUCTIONS
SQUARE

Rnd 1: With size H hook, ch 8, sl st in first ch to form ring, ch 3 *(counts as first dc)*, 31 dc in ring, **join** *(see Pattern Notes)* in 3rd ch of beg ch-3. *(32 dc)*

Rnd 2: Ch 7, sk next 3 sts, [sl st in next st, ch 7, sk next 3 sts] around, ending with ch 3, sk last 3 sts, join with dc in beg ch of beg ch-7 forming last ch sp.

Rnd 3: Ch 3, 6 dc in same ch sp, 7 dc in center ch of each ch-7 sp around, join in 3rd ch of beg ch-3. Fasten off.

Rnd 4: Join in center dc of any dc group, ch 7 *(counts as first tr and ch-3)*, tr in same st *(corner)*, *ch 3, **dc dec** *(see Stitch Guide)* in 5th dc of this dc group and 2nd dc of next dc group, ch 3, sk next st, sc in next st, ch 3, sk next st, dc dec in next st and 2nd dc of next dc group, ch 3, sk next st**, (tr, ch 3, tr) in next st, rep from * around, ending last rep at **, join in 4th ch of beg ch-7.

Rnd 5: Sl st in first ch sp, ch 1, 6 sc in same ch sp, *sc in next st, [3 sc in next ch sp, sc in next st] 4 times**, 6 sc in next ch sp, rep from * around, ending last rep at **, join in beg sc. Fasten off. ■

Square 9

FINISHED SIZE
7½ inches square

GAUGE
Rnds 1 & 2 = 3 inches

PATTERN NOTES
Join with slip stitch as indicated unless otherwise stated.

Chain-3 at beginning of row or round counts as first double crochet unless otherwise stated.

Square is made with 1 color of medium (worsted) weight yarn.

SPECIAL STITCHES
Beginning cluster (beg cl): Ch 3 *(counts as first dc)*, holding last lp of each st on hook, 3 dc in place indicated, yo, pull through all lps on hook.

Cluster (cl): Holding last lp of each st on hook, 4 dc in place indicated, yo, pull through all lps on hook.

INSTRUCTIONS
SQUARE
Rnd 1: With size H hook, ch 6, sl st in first ch to form ring, ch 3, 11 dc in ring, **join** *(see Pattern Notes)* in 3rd ch of beg ch-3. *(12 dc)*

Rnd 2: **Beg cl** *(see Special Stitches)* in first st, [ch 1, **cl** *(see Special Stitches)* in next st] twice, ch 5, *[cl in next st, ch 1] twice, cl in next st, ch 5, rep from * around, join in top of beg cl.

Rnd 3: Sl st in next ch sp, beg cl in same ch sp, *ch 1, cl in next ch sp, ch 2, 5 dc in next ch sp, ch 2**, cl in next ch sp, rep from * around, ending last rep at **, join in top of beg cl.

Rnd 4: Sl st in next ch sp, beg cl in same ch sp, *ch 2, dc in next ch sp, dc in each of next 2 sts, 5 dc in next st, dc in each of next 2 sts, dc in next ch sp, ch 2**, cl in next ch sp, rep from * around, ending last rep at **, join in top of beg cl.

Rnd 5: Ch 3, *2 dc in next ch sp, dc in each of next 4 sts, ch 3, sk next st, cl in next st, ch 3, sk next st, dc in each of next 4 sts, 2 dc in next ch sp**, dc in next st, rep from * around, ending last rep at **, join in 3rd ch of beg ch-3.

Rnd 6: Ch 3, dc in each of next 6 sts, *ch 2, cl in next ch sp, ch 5, cl in next ch sp**, dc in each of next 13 sts, rep from * around, ending last rep at **, dc in each rem st around, join in 3rd ch of beg ch-3. Fasten off. ■

Square 10

Rnd 3: Ch 3, *5 dc in next st, dc in next st, ch 2, sk next ch sp, dc in next st, ch 2, sk next ch sp**, dc in next st, rep from * around, ending last rep at **, join in 3rd ch of beg ch-3.

Rnd 4: Ch 3, dc in each of next 2 sts, *5 dc in next st, dc in each of next 3 sts, ch 2, sk next ch sp, dc in next st, ch 2, sk next ch sp**, dc in each of next 3 sts, rep from * around, ending last rep at **, join in 3rd ch of beg ch-3.

Rnd 5: Ch 3, dc in each of next 4 sts, *5 dc in next st, dc in each of next 5 sts, 2 dc in next ch sp, dc in next st, 2 dc in next ch sp**, dc in each of next 5 sts, rep from * around, ending last rep at **, join in 3rd ch of beg ch-3. Fasten off. ∎

FINISHED SIZE
5¾ inches square

GAUGE
Rnds 1 & 2 = 3 inches

PATTERN NOTES
Join with slip stitch as indicated unless otherwise stated.

Chain-3 at beginning of row or round counts as first double crochet unless otherwise stated.

Square is made with 1 color of medium (worsted) weight yarn.

INSTRUCTIONS
SQUARE
Rnd 1: With size H hook, ch 6, sl st in first ch to form ring, **ch 3** (see Pattern Notes), 15 dc in ring, **join** (see Pattern Notes) in 3rd ch of beg ch-3. (16 dc)

Rnd 2: Ch 3, *2 dc in next st, ch 2, sk next st, dc in next st, ch 2, sk next st**, dc in next st, rep from * around, ending last rep at **, join in 3rd ch of beg ch-3.

Square 11

FINISHED SIZE
8 inches square

GAUGE
Rnds 1–3 = 4 inches

PATTERN NOTES
Join with slip stitch as indicated unless otherwise stated.

Chain-3 at beginning of row or round counts as first double crochet unless otherwise stated.

Square is made with 4 colors and medium (worsted) weight yarn.

INSTRUCTIONS
SQUARE
Rnd 1: With size H hook, ch 4, 2 dc in 4th ch from hook (*first 3 chs count as first dc*), ch 2, [3 dc in same ch, ch 2] 3 times, **join** (*see Pattern Notes*) in 3rd ch of beg ch-3. Fasten off. (*12 dc*)

Rnd 2: Join next color in any ch sp, **ch 3** (*see Pattern Notes*), (2 dc, ch 2, 3 dc) in same ch sp (*corner*), ch 1, [(3 dc, ch 2, 3 dc) in next ch sp (*corner*), ch 1] around, join in 3rd ch of beg ch-3. Fasten off.

Rnd 3: Join next color in any ch-2 sp, ch 3, (2 dc, ch 2, 3 dc) in same ch sp, ch 1, *3 dc in next ch sp, ch 1**, (3 dc, ch 2, 3 dc) in next ch sp, ch 1, rep from * around, ending last rep at **, join in 3rd ch of beg ch-3. Fasten off.

Rnd 4: Join next color with sc in any corner ch sp, ch 5, sc in same ch sp, *[ch 5, sc in next ch sp] twice**, ch 5, (sc, ch 5, sc) in corner ch sp, rep from * around, ending last rep at **, ch 2, join with dc in beg sc forming last ch sp.

Rnd 5: Ch 1, sc in this ch sp, ch 1, *9 dc in corner ch sp, ch 1, sc in next ch sp**, [ch 5, sc in next ch sp] twice, ch 1, rep from * around, ending last rep at **, ch 5, sc in next ch sp, ch 2, join with dc in beg sc forming last ch sp.

Rnd 6: Ch 1, sc in this ch sp, *ch 5, sk next ch sp and next st, sc in next st, ch 5, sk next 2 sts, (sc, ch 5, sc) in next st, ch 5, sk next 2 sts, sc in next st, ch 5, sk next st and next ch sp, sc in next ch sp, ch 5**, sc in next ch sp, rep from * around, ending last rep at **, join with sl st in beg sc. Fasten off.

Rnd 7: Join 3rd color with sl st in any corner ch-5 sp, ch 3, (2 dc, ch 2, 3 dc) in same ch sp, *ch 1, [3 dc in next ch sp, ch 1] 5 times**, (3 dc, ch 2, 3 dc) in next corner ch sp, rep from * around, ending last rep at **, join in 3rd ch of beg ch-3. Fasten off. ∎

Square 12

FINISHED SIZE
7 inches square

GAUGE
Rnds 1 & 2 = 3¼ inches

PATTERN NOTES
Join with slip stitch as indicated unless otherwise stated.

Square is made with 3 colors of medium (worsted) weight yarn.

SPECIAL STITCHES
Beginning cluster (beg cl): Ch 3 (*counts as first dc*), holding back last lp of each st on hook, 2 dc in place indicated, yo, pull through all lps on hook.

Cluster (cl): Holding back last lp of each st on hook, 3 dc in place indicated, yo, pull through all lps on hook.

INSTRUCTIONS
SQUARE
Rnd 1: With size H hook, ch 4, sl st in first ch to form ring, ch 4 (*counts as first dc and ch-1*), [dc in ring, ch 1] 11 times, **join** (*see Pattern Notes*) in 3rd ch of beg ch-4. Fasten off. (*12 dc*)

Rnd 2: Join next color in any ch sp, **beg cl** (see Special Stitches) in same ch sp, ch 3, [**cl** (see Special Stitches) in next ch sp, ch 3] around, join in beg cl. Fasten off.

Rnd 3: Join first color with sc in any ch sp, ch 5, [sc in next ch sp, ch 5] around, join in beg sc. Fasten off.

Rnd 4: Join next color with sc in any ch sp, *ch 5, sc in next ch sp, ch 1, (5 dc, ch 3, 5 dc) in next ch sp (corner), ch 1**, sc in next ch sp, rep from * around, ending last rep at **, join in beg sc. **Do not fasten off.**

Rnd 5: Ch 3 (counts as first dc), *3 dc in next ch sp, dc in next st, dc in next ch sp, dc in each of next 5 sts, (dc, ch 3, dc) in next ch sp (corner), dc in each of next 5 sts, dc in next ch sp**, dc in next st, rep from * around, ending last rep at **, join in 3rd ch of beg ch-3. Fasten off.

Rnd 6: Join first color with sc in any corner ch sp, ch 5, sc in same ch sp, *sc in next st, [ch 3, sk next st, sc in next st] 9 times**, (sc, ch 5, sc) in next corner ch sp, rep from * around, ending last rep at **, join in beg sc. Fasten off. ■

Square 13

FINISHED SIZE
6½ inches square

GAUGE
Rnds 1 & 2 = 3 inches

PATTERN NOTES
Chain-3 at beginning of row or round counts as first double crochet unless otherwise stated.

Join with slip stitch as indicated unless otherwise stated.

Square is made with 2 colors and medium (worsted) weight yarn.

INSTRUCTIONS
SQUARE
Rnd 1: Ch 4, sl st in first ch to form ring, **ch 3** (see Pattern Notes), 2 dc in ring, ch 8, [3 dc in ring, ch 8] 3 times, **join** (see Pattern Notes) in 3rd ch of beg ch-3.

Rnd 2: Ch 3, ***fpdc** (see Stitch Guide) around next st, dc in next st, ch 8**, dc in next st, rep from * around, ending last rep at **, join in 3rd ch of beg ch-3. Fasten off.

Rnd 3: Join next color in first st, ch 3, dc in each of next 2 sts, ch 1, working over both ch-8 sps at same time, (3 dc, ch 3, 3 dc, ch 1) in next ch-8 sp (corner), *dc in each of next 3 sts, ch 1, working over both ch-8 sps at same time, (3 dc, ch 3, 3 dc) in next ch-8 sp (corner), ch 1, rep from * around, join in 3rd ch of beg ch-3. Fasten off.

Rnd 4: Join first color in ch-1 sp to right of joining, ch 3, ***fpdtr** (see Stitch Guide) around dc 2 rnds below, sk st behind fpdtr on this rnd, dc in next st on this rnd, fpdtr around next st 2 rnds below, sk st behind fpdtr on this rnd, dc in next ch-1 sp, dc in each of next 3 sts, (2 dc, ch 3, 2 dc) in next ch-3 sp (corner), dc in each of next 3 sts**, dc in next ch-1 sp, rep from * around, ending last rep at **, join in 3rd ch of beg ch-3. Fasten off.

Rnd 5: Join 2nd color in any corner ch sp, ch 7 (counts as first dc and ch-4), dc in same ch sp, *dc in each of next 6 sts, ch 1, sk next fpdtr,

fpdtr around next st 2 rnds below, sk st behind fpdtr on this rnd, ch 1, sk next st, dc in each of next 6 sts**, (dc, ch 4, dc) in next corner ch sp, rep from * around, ending last rep at **, join in 3rd ch of beg ch-7. Fasten off.

Rnd 6: Join first color with sc in any corner ch sp, 4 sc in same ch sp, *sc in each st and in each ch across to next corner ch sp**, 5 sc in corner ch sp, rep from * around, ending last rep at **, join in beg sc. Fasten off. ■

Square 14

FINISHED SIZE
6¾ inches square

GAUGE
Rnds 1–3 = 4 inches

PATTERN NOTES
Chain-3 at beginning of row or round counts as first double crochet unless otherwise stated.

Join with slip stitch as indicated unless otherwise stated.

Square is made with 4 colors of medium (worsted) weight yarn.

INSTRUCTIONS
SQUARE
Rnd 1: With size H hook, ch 4, sl st in first ch to form ring, **ch 3** *(see Pattern Notes)*, 3 dc in ring, ch 2, [4 dc in ring, ch 2] 3 times, **join** *(see Pattern Note)* in 3rd ch of beg ch-3. Fasten off. *(16 dc)*

Rnd 2: Join next color with sc in any ch sp, (sc, ch 2, 2 sc) in same ch sp *(corner)*, *sc in each of next 4 sts**, (2 sc, ch 2, 2 sc) in next ch sp *(corner)*, rep from * around, ending last rep at **, join in beg sc. Fasten off.

Rnd 3: Join next color with sc in any corner ch sp, (sc, ch 2, 2 sc) in same ch sp, *sk next 4 sts, (3 dc, ch 2, 3 dc) in sp between 4th and 5th sts**, (2 sc, ch 2, 2 sc) in next corner ch sp, rep from * around, ending last rep at **, join in beg sc. Fasten off.

Rnd 4: Join next color in any corner ch sp, ch 2 *(counts as first hdc)*, (hdc, ch 2, 2 hdc) in same ch sp, *sc in each of next 5 sts, 3 sc in next ch sp, sc in each of next 5 sts**, (2 hdc, ch 2, 2 hdc) in next corner ch sp, rep from * around, ending last rep at **, join in 2nd ch of beg ch-2. Fasten off.

Rnd 5: Join 2nd color in any corner ch-2 sp, ch 2, (hdc, ch 2, 2 hdc) in same ch sp, *sk next st, hdc in each of next 6 sts, sk next st, sc in next st, sk next st, hdc in each of next 6 sts, sk next st**, (2 hdc, ch 2, 2 hdc) in next corner ch sp, rep from * around, ending last rep at **, join in 2nd ch of beg ch-2. Fasten off.

Rnd 6: Join 3rd color in any corner ch sp, ch 3, (dc, ch 2, 2 dc) in same ch sp, *dc in each of next 8 sts, working over next sc, dc in ch sp 2 rnds below, dc in each of next 8 sts**, (2 dc, ch 2, 2 dc) in next corner ch sp, rep from * around, ending last rep at **, join in 3rd ch of beg ch-3. Fasten off.

Rnd 7: Join first color with sc in any corner ch sp, 2 sc in same ch sp, sc in each st around with 3 sc in each corner ch sp, join in beg sc. Fasten off. ■

Square 15

FINISHED SIZE
6½ inches

GAUGE
Rnds 1 & 2 = 2¾ inches

PATTERN NOTES
Chain-3 at beginning of row or round counts as first double crochet unless otherwise stated.

Join with slip stitch as indicated unless otherwise stated.

Square is made with 1 color of medium (worsted) weight yarn.

SPECIAL STITCH
Puff stitch (puff st): [Yo, insert hook in st, yo, pull lp through] 3 times, yo, pull through all lps on hook.

INSTRUCTIONS
SQUARE
Rnd 1: With size H hook, ch 4, sl st in first ch to form ring, **ch 3** (see Pattern Notes), 11 dc in ring, **join** (see Pattern Notes) in 3rd ch of beg ch-3. (12 dc)

Rnd 2: **Puff st** (see Special Stitch) in first st, *[ch 1, puff st in next st] twice, ch 5 (corner)**, puff st in next st, rep from * around, ending last rep at **, join in beg puff st.

Rnd 3: *[Puff st in next ch sp, ch 1] twice, 5 dc in next ch sp, ch 1, rep from * around, join in beg puff st.

Rnd 4: [Puff st in next ch sp, ch 1, dc in next ch sp, dc in each of next 2 sts, 3 dc in next st (corner), dc in each of next 2 sts, dc in next ch sp, ch 1] around, join in beg puff st.

Rnd 5: Sl st in next ch sp, ch 4 (counts as first dc and ch-1), *[sk next st, dc in next st, ch 1] twice, (2 dc, ch 1, 2 dc) in next st (corner), ch 1, dc in next st, ch 1, sk next st, dc in next st**, [ch 1, sk next st, dc in next ch sp] twice, ch 1, rep from * around, ending last rep at **, ch 1, sk next st, dc in next ch sp, ch 1, sk last st, join in 3rd ch of beg ch-4.

Rnd 6: Sl st in next ch sp, ch 4, [sk next st, dc in next ch sp, ch 1] twice, *sk next 2 sts, (2 dc, ch 3, 2 dc) in corner ch sp, ch 1, sk next 2 sts**, [dc in next ch sp, ch 1, sk next st] 6 times, dc in next ch sp, ch 1, rep from * around, ending last rep at **, [dc in next ch sp, ch 1, sk next st] across, join in 3rd ch of beg ch-4. Fasten off. ∎

Square 16

FINISHED SIZE
8½ inches square

GAUGE
Rnds 1 & 2 = 3 inches

PATTERN NOTES
Join with slip stitch as indicated unless otherwise stated.

Chain-3 at beginning of row or round counts as first double crochet unless otherwise stated.

Square is made with 3 colors of medium (worsted) weight yarn.

INSTRUCTIONS
SQUARE
Rnd 1: With size H hook, ch 4, sl st in first ch to form ring, ch 6 *(counts as first dc and ch-3)*, [3 dc in ring, ch 3] 3 times, 2 dc in ring, **join** *(see Pattern Notes)* in 3rd ch of beg ch-6.

Rnd 2: Sl st in first ch sp, **ch 3** *(see Pattern Notes)*, (2 dc, ch 3, 3 dc) in same ch sp *(corner)*, *dc in next st, **fpdc** *(see Stitch Guide)* around next st, dc in next st**, (3 dc, ch 3, 3 dc) in next ch sp *(corner)*, rep from * around, ending last rep at **, join in 3rd ch of beg ch-3.

Rnd 3: Sl st in each of next 2 sts, sl st in next ch sp, ch 3, (2 dc, ch 3, 3 dc) in same ch sp, *dc in each of next 4 sts, fpdc around next fpdc, dc in each of next 4 sts**, (3 dc, ch 3, 3 dc) in next ch sp, rep from * around, ending last rep at **, join in 3rd ch of beg ch-3. Fasten off.

Rnd 4: Join next color in any ch sp, ch 3, 2 dc in same ch sp, *fpdc around next st, dc in each of next 6 sts, fpdc around next fpdc, dc in each of next 6 sts, fpdc around next st**, 3 dc in next ch sp, rep from * around, ending last rep at **, join in 3rd ch of beg ch-3.

Rnd 5: Ch 3, *3 dc in next st, dc in next st, fpdc around next fpdc, dc in each of next 6 sts, fpdc around next fpdc, dc in each of next 6 sts, fpdc around next fpdc**, dc in next st, rep from * around, ending last rep at **, join in 3rd ch of beg ch-3. Fasten off.

Rnd 6: Join next color in any center corner st,
ch 3, 2 dc in same st, *dc in each of next 2 sts, fpdc around next fpdc, dc in each of next 6 sts, fpdc around next fpdc, dc in each of next 6 sts, fpdc around next fpdc, dc in each of next 2 sts**, 3 dc in next st, rep from * around, ending last rep at **, join in 3rd ch of beg ch-3. Fasten off.

Rnd 7: Join first color with sc in first st, ***fptr** *(see Stitch Guide)* around next st 2 rnds below, sc in st behind fptr, sc in each of next 3 sts, fpdc around next fpdc, sc in each of next 6 sts, fpdc around next fpdc, sc in each of next 6 sts, fpdc around next st**, sc in each of next 3 sts, rep from * around, ending last rep at **, sc in each of last 2 sts, join in beg sc. Fasten off. ∎

Square 17

FINISHED SIZE
5¾ inches square

GAUGE
Rnds 1 & 2 = 3½ inches

PATTERN NOTES
Join with slip stitch as indicated unless otherwise stated.

Chain-3 at beginning of row or round counts as first double crochet unless otherwise stated.

Square is made with 2 colors of medium (worsted) weight yarn.

SPECIAL STITCHES
Beginning cluster (beg cl): Ch 2 *(counts as first hdc)*, holding back last lp of each st on hook, 3 dc in place indicated, yo, pull through all lps on hook.

Cluster (cl): Holding back last lp of each st on hook, 4 dc in place indicated, yo, pull through all lps on hook.

INSTRUCTIONS
SQUARE
Rnd 1: With size H hook, ch 4, sl st in first ch to form ring, ch 4 *(counts as first dc and ch-1)*, [dc in ring, ch 1] 11 times, **join** *(see Pattern Notes)* in 3rd ch of beg ch-4. *(12 dc)*

Rnd 2: Sl st in first ch sp, **beg cl** *(see Special Stitches)* in same ch sp, ch 1, [**cl** *(see Special Stitches)* in next ch sp, ch 1] around, join in beg cl. Fasten off.

Rnd 3: Join next color with sc in any ch sp, *[ch 5, sc in next ch sp] twice, ch 7**, sc in next ch sp, rep from * around, ending last rep at **, join in beg sc. Fasten off.

Rnd 4: Join first color in any ch-7 sp, **ch 3** *(see Pattern Notes)*, (2 dc, 3 tr, ch 2, 3 tr, 3 dc) in same ch sp *(corner)*, *sc in next ch-5 sp, ch 3, sc in next ch-5 sp**, (3 dc, 3 tr, ch 2, 3 tr, 3 dc) in next ch-7 sp *(corner)*, rep from * around, ending last rep at **, join in 3rd ch of beg ch-3. Fasten off.

Rnd 5: Join 2nd color with sc in any corner ch-2 sp, 2 sc in same ch sp, *sc in each of next 3 sts, hdc in each of next 3 sts, sk next st, 3 dc in next ch sp, sk next st, hdc in each of next 3 sts, sc in each of next 3 sts**, 3 sc in next ch sp, rep from * around, ending last rep at **, join in beg sc. Fasten off. ■

Square 18

FINISHED SIZE
6½ inches square

GAUGE
Rnds 1 & 2 = 3 inches

PATTERN NOTES
Join with slip stitch as indicated unless otherwise stated.

Chain-3 at beginning of row or round counts as first double crochet unless otherwise stated.

Square is made with 3 colors of medium (worsted) weight yarn.

SPECIAL STITCH
Cluster (cl): [Yo, insert hook in ch sp, yo, pull lp through, yo, pull through 2 lps on hook] twice, yo twice, insert hook around st 2 rnds below, yo, pull lp through [yo, pull through 2 lps on hook] twice, [yo, insert hook in same ch sp, yo, pull lp through, yo, pull through 2 lps on hook] twice, yo, pull through all lps on hook.

INSTRUCTIONS
SQUARE
Rnd 1: With size H hook, ch 4, sl st in first ch

to form ring, **ch 3** *(see Pattern Notes)*, 2 dc in ring, ch 3, [3 dc in ring, ch 3] 3 times, **join** *(see Pattern Notes)* in 3rd ch of beg ch-3.

Rnd 2: Sl st across to first ch sp, ch 3, (2 dc, ch 3, 3 dc) in same ch sp *(corner)*, *ch 1, sk next 3 sts**, (3 dc, ch 3, 3 dc) in next ch sp *(corner)*, rep from * around, ending last rep at **, join in 3rd ch of beg ch-3. Fasten off.

Rnd 3: Join next color in any corner ch sp, ch 3, (2 dc, ch 3, 3 dc) in same ch sp, *ch 1, **cl** *(see Special Stitch)*, ch 1**, (3 dc, ch 3, 3 dc) in next corner ch sp, rep from * around, ending last rep at **, join in 3rd ch of beg ch-3. Fasten off.

Rnd 4: Join next color in any corner ch sp, ch 3, (2 dc, ch 3, 3 dc) in same ch sp, *[ch 3, cl] twice, ch 3**, (3 dc, ch 3, 3 dc) in next ch sp, rep from * around, ending last rep at **, join in 3rd ch of beg ch-3. Fasten off.

Rnd 5: Join first color in any corner ch sp, ch 3, (2 dc, ch 3, 3 dc) in same ch sp, *ch 3, 3 dc in next ch sp, ch 3, cl, ch 3, 3 dc in next ch sp, ch 3**, (3 dc, ch 3, 3 dc) in next ch sp, rep from * around, ending last rep at **, join with sl st in 3rd ch of beg ch-3. Fasten off. ∎

Square 19

PATTERN NOTES

Join with slip stitch as indicated unless otherwise stated.

Chain-3 at beginning of row or round counts as first double crochet unless otherwise stated.

Square is made with 2 colors of medium (worsted) weight yarn.

SPECIAL STITCHES

Beginning popcorn (beg pc): Ch 3 *(counts as first dc)*, 4 dc in same place, drop lp from hook, insert hook in 3rd ch of beg ch-3, pull dropped lp through, ch 1 to secure.

Popcorn (pc): 5 dc in place indicated, drop lp from hook, insert hook in first dc of group, pull dropped lp through, ch 1 to secure.

INSTRUCTIONS
SQUARE

Rnd 1: With size H hook, ch 4, sl st in first ch to form ring, **beg pc** *(see Special Stitches)*, ch 5, [**pc** *(see Special Stitches)* in ring, ch 5] 7 times, **join** *(see Pattern Notes)* in beg pc. Fasten off. *(8 ch sps)*

Rnd 2: Join next color in any ch sp, **ch 3** *(see Pattern Notes)*, 2 dc in same ch sp, *ch 2, (pc, ch 3, pc) in next ch sp *(corner)*, ch 2**, 3 dc in next ch sp, rep from * around, ending last rep at **, join in 3rd ch of beg ch-3. Fasten off.

Rnd 3: Join first color in any corner ch sp, (beg pc, ch 3, pc) in same ch sp, *ch 2, 2 dc in next ch sp, dc in each of next 3 sts, 2 dc in next ch sp, ch 2**, (pc, ch 3, pc) in next corner ch sp, rep from * around, ending last rep at **, join in beg pc. Fasten off.

Rnd 4: Join 2nd color in any corner ch sp, (beg pc, ch 2, 2 tr, ch 2, pc) in same ch sp, *pc in next ch sp, [sk next st, pc in next st] 3 times, sk next st, pc in next ch sp**, (pc, ch 2, 2 tr, ch 2, pc) in next corner ch sp, rep from * around, ending last rep at **, join in beg pc. Fasten off. ∎

Square 20

FINISHED SIZE
7½ inches square

GAUGE
Rnds 1–3 = 4 inches

PATTERN NOTES
Join with slip stitch as indicated unless otherwise stated.

Chain-3 at beginning of row or round counts as first double crochet unless otherwise stated.

Square is made with 3 colors of medium (worsted) weight yarn.

SPECIAL STITCHES
Beginning treble cluster (beg tr cl): Ch 4 *(counts as first tr)*, holding back last lp of each st on hook, 3 tr in place indicated, yo, pull through all lps on hook.

Treble cluster (tr cl): Holding back last lp of each st on hook, 4 tr in place indicated, yo, pull through all lps on hook.

Beginning double crochet cluster (beg dc cl): Ch 3 *(counts as first dc)*, holding back last lp of each st on hook, 2 dc in place indicated, yo, pull through all lps on hook.

Double crochet cluster (dc cl): Holding back last lp of each st on hook, 3 dc in place indicated, yo, pull through all lps on hook.

INSTRUCTIONS
SQUARE
Rnd 1: With size H hook, ch 2, 8 sc in 2nd ch from hook, **join** *(see Pattern Notes)* in beg sc.

Rnd 2: **Beg tr cl** *(see Special Stitches)* in first st, ch 2, **tr cl** *(see Special Stitches)* in same st, ch 3, sk next st, [(tr cl, ch 2, tr cl) in next st, ch 3, sk next st] around, join in beg tr cl. Fasten off.

Rnd 3: Join next color with sc in any ch-3 sp, **beg dc cl** *(see Special Stitches)* in same ch sp, ch 3, **dc cl** *(see Special Stitches)* in same ch sp, *ch 1, (sc, ch 2, sc) in next ch sp, ch 1**, (dc cl, ch 3, dc cl) in next ch sp, rep from * around, ending last rep at **, join in beg dc cl. Fasten off.

Rnd 4: Join next color in any ch-2 sp, ch 4 *(counts as first tr)*, 4 tr in same ch sp *(corner)*, *2 dc in next ch sp, ch 1, 3 dc in next ch sp, ch 1, 2 dc in next ch sp**, 5 tr in next ch sp *(corner)*, rep from * around, ending last rep at **, join in 4th ch of beg ch-4. Fasten off.

Rnd 5: Join 2nd color with sc in any center corner tr, 4 sc in same st, *[sk next st, 2 sc in next st] twice, sk next ch sp, 2 sc in next st, sk next st, 2 sc in next st, sk next ch sp, [2 sc in next st, sk next st] twice**, 5 sc in center corner st, rep from * around, ending last rep at **, join in beg sc. Fasten off.

Rnd 6: Join first color with sc in sk st on rnd 4 before any corner tr group, *ch 5, sk next 5 sc in corner, [sc in next sk st on rnd 4, ch 3] 6 times**, sc in next sk st on rnd 4, rep from * around, ending last rep at **, join in beg sc.

Rnd 7: Sl st in first ch-5 sp, (beg dc cl, {ch 1, dc cl} twice) in same ch sp, *[ch 1, 2 dc in next ch sp] 6 times, ch 2**, (dc cl, {ch 2, dc cl} twice) in next ch-5 sp, rep from * around, ending last rep at **, join in beg dc cl. Fasten off.

Rnd 8: Join 2nd color with sc in any ch sp, ch 2, [sc in next ch sp, ch 2] around, join in beg sc. Fasten off. ■

Square 21

FINISHED SIZE
8 inches square

GAUGE
Rnds 1–3 = 4 inches

PATTERN NOTES
Join with slip stitch as indicated unless otherwise stated.

Chain-3 at beginning of row or round counts as first double crochet unless otherwise stated.

Square is made with 3 colors of medium (worsted) weight yarn.

SPECIAL STITCH
Cluster (cl): Ch 3 *(counts as first dc)*, holding back last lp of each st on hook, 3 dc in 3rd ch from hook, yo, pull through all lps on hook, ch 1.

INSTRUCTIONS
SQUARE
Rnd 1: With size H hook, ch 4, sl st in first ch to form ring, **ch 3** *(see Pattern Notes)*, 2 dc in ring, ch 3, [3 dc in ring, ch 3] 3 times, **join** *(see Pattern Notes)* in 3rd ch of beg ch-3. Fasten off.

Rnd 2: Join next color in any ch sp, ch 3, (2 dc, ch 3, 3 dc) in same ch sp, ch 1, [(3 dc, ch 3, 3 dc) in next ch sp, ch 1] around, join in 3rd ch of beg ch-3. Fasten off.

Rnd 3: Join next color in any ch-3 sp, ch 3, (2 dc, ch 3, 3 dc) in same ch sp *(corner)*, *ch 1, 3 dc in next ch sp, ch 1**, (3 dc, ch 3, 3 dc) in next ch sp *(corner)*, rep from * around, ending last rep at **, join in 3rd ch of beg ch-3. Fasten off.

Rnd 4: Join first color in any corner ch sp, (**cl**—*see Special Stitch*, sc) in same ch sp, *[cl, sc in next ch sp] twice, cl**, (sc, cl, sc) in next corner ch sp, rep from * around, ending last rep at **, join in beg sc. Fasten off.

Rnd 5: Fold cl to front, working in sts on rnd 3 behind cl, join 3rd color in any corner ch sp between sc on rnd 4, ch 3, (2 dc, ch 3, 3 dc) in same ch sp, *[ch 1, dc in each of next 3 sts on rnd 3] 3 times, ch 1**, (3 dc, ch 3, 3 dc) in next corner ch sp between sc on rnd 4, rep from * around, ending last rep at **, join in 3rd ch of beg ch-3. Fasten off.

Rnd 6: Join 2nd color in any corner ch sp, ch 3, (2 dc, ch 3, 3 dc) in same ch sp, *[ch 1, 3 dc in next ch sp] 4 times, ch 1**, (3 dc, ch 3, 3 dc) in next corner ch sp, rep from * around, ending last rep at **, join in 3rd ch of beg ch-3. Fasten off.

Rnd 7: Join 3rd color with sc in any corner ch sp, 2 sc in same ch sp, sc in each st and in each ch around with 3 sc in each corner ch sp, join in beg sc. Fasten off.

Rnd 8: Join first color with sc in any center corner st, (tr, sc) in same st, *[tr in next st, sc in next st] across to next center corner st**, (sc, tr, sc) in center corner st, rep from * around, ending last rep at **, join in beg sc. Fasten off. ■

Square 22

FINISHED SIZE
5½ inches square

GAUGE
Rnds 1–3 = 3½ inches

PATTERN NOTES
Join with slip stitch as indicated unless otherwise stated.

Chain-3 at beginning of row or round counts as first double crochet unless otherwise stated.

Square is made with 2 colors of medium (worsted) weight yarn.

SPECIAL STITCH
Cluster (cl): Holding back last lp of each st on hook, 5 dc in place indicated, yo, pull through all lps on hook.

INSTRUCTIONS
SQUARE
Rnd 1: With size H hook, ch 4, sl st in first ch to form ring, **ch 3** (see Pattern Notes), 4 dc in ring, ch 2, [5 dc in ring, ch 2] 3 times, **join** (see Pattern Notes) in 3rd ch of beg ch-3. Fasten off.

Rnd 2: Join next color with sc in any ch sp, 2 sc in same ch sp (corner), sc in each st around with 3 sc in each ch sp (corner), join in beg sc. Fasten off.

Rnd 3: Join first color with sc in center corner st, 2 sc in same st, *sc in next st, **cl** (see Special Stitch) in next st, sc in next st, **fpdc** (see Stitch Guide) around next st on rnd before last, sk st behind fpdc on this rnd, sc in next st, cl in next st, sc in next st**, 3 sc in next st (corner), rep from * around, ending last rep at **, join in beg sc.

Rnd 4: Ch 1, sc in first st, 3 sc in next st (corner), *sc in each st across to next center corner st**, 3 sc in corner st, rep from * around, ending last rep at **, join in beg sc. Fasten off.

Rnd 5: Join 2nd color in any center corner st, ch 3, 2 dc in same st, *dc in each st across to next center corner st**, 3 dc in corner st, rep from * around, ending last rep at **, join in 3rd ch of beg ch-3. Fasten off.

Rnd 6: Join first color with sc in any center corner st, 2 sc in same corner, *sc in each of next 6 sts, cl in next st, sc in each of next 6 sts**, 3 sc in next st, rep from * around, ending last rep at **, join in beg sc. Fasten off.

Rnd 7: Join 2nd color with sc in any center corner st, 2 sc in same st, sc in each st around with 3 sc in each center corner st, join in beg sc. Fasten off. ■

Square 23

FINISHED SIZE
7¼ inches square

GAUGE
Rnds 1–3 = 3 inches

PATTERN NOTES
Join with slip stitch as indicated unless otherwise stated.

Chain-3 at beginning of row or round counts as first double crochet unless otherwise stated.

Square is made with 3 colors of medium (worsted) weight yarn.

INSTRUCTIONS
SQUARE
Rnd 1: With size H hook, ch 4, sl st in first ch to form ring, ch 4 *(counts as first dc and ch-1)*, [dc in ring, ch 1] 7 times, **join** *(see Pattern Notes)* in 3rd ch of beg ch-4.

Rnd 2: Sl st in first ch sp, **ch 3** *(see Pattern Notes)*, (dc, ch 3, 2 dc) in same ch sp *(corner)*, ch 1, sk next ch sp, [(2 dc, ch 3, 2 dc) in next ch sp *(corner)*, ch 1, sk next ch sp] around, join in 3rd ch of beg ch-3. Fasten off.

Rnd 3: Join next color with sc in any corner ch sp, 2 sc in same ch sp, *sc in each of next 2 sts, ch 2, sk next ch sp, sc in each of next 2 sts**, 3 sc in next ch sp, rep from * around, ending last rep at **, join in beg sc. Fasten off.

Rnd 4: Join next color with sc in any center corner st, 2 sc in same st, *sc in each of next 3 sts, working behind ch-2, dc in ch sp on rnd 2, sc in each of next 3 sts**, 3 sc in next st, rep from * around, ending last rep at **, join in beg sc. Fasten off.

Rnd 5: Join first color in first sc of corner group, ch 3, *(dc, ch 3, dc) in next st *(corner)*, dc in next st**, [ch 1, sk next st, dc in next st] 4 times, (dc, ch 3, dc) in next st *(corner)*, rep from * around, ending last rep at **, ch 1, sk next st, [dc in next st, ch 1, sk next st] across, join in 3rd ch of beg ch-3. Fasten off.

Rnd 6: Join 2nd color with sc in any corner ch sp, 2 sc in same ch sp, *sc in each of next 2 sts, sc in next ch sp, sc in next st, working in front of sts of last 2 rnds, 3 tr in ch-2 sp on rnd 3, sk next ch sp, next st and next ch sp behind 3 tr on this rnd, sc in next st, sc in next ch sp, sc in each of next 2 sts**, 3 sc in next ch sp, rep from * around, ending last rep at **, join in beg sc. Fasten off.

Rnd 7: Join 3rd color with sc in any center corner st, 2 sc in same st, *sc in each of next 5 sts, ch 3, sk next 3 tr, sc in each of next 5 sts**, 3 sc in next st, rep from * around, ending last rep at **, join in beg sc. Fasten off.

Rnd 8: Join first color in center corner sc, ch 3, 4 dc in same st, *dc in each of next 6 sts, 3 dc in next ch sp, dc in each of next 6 sts**, 5 dc in center corner st, rep from * around, ending last rep at **, join in 3rd ch of beg ch-3. Fasten off.

Rnd 9: Join 2nd color in any center corner st, ch 3, 2 dc in same st, dc in each st around with 3 dc in each center corner st, join in 3rd ch of beg ch-3. Fasten off. ∎

Square 24

FINISHED SIZE
6 inches square

GAUGE
Rnds 1–3 = 3¼ inches

PATTERN NOTES
Join with slip stitch as indicated unless otherwise stated.

Chain-3 at beginning of row or round counts as first double crochet unless otherwise stated.

Square is made with 4 colors of medium (worsted) weight yarn.

SPECIAL STITCH
Cluster (cl): Ch 3, holding back last lp of each st on hook, 3 dc in 3rd ch from hook, yo, pull through all lps on hook, ch 1.

INSTRUCTIONS
SQUARE
Rnd 1: With size H hook, ch 4, sl st in first ch to form ring, **ch 3** *(see Pattern Notes)*, 2 dc in ring, ch 3, [3 dc in ring, ch 3] 3 times, **join** *(see Pattern Notes)* in 3rd ch of beg ch-3, **turn.** Fasten off.

Rnd 2: Ch 1, (sc, **cl**—*see Special Stitch*, sc) in first ch sp, cl, [(sc, cl, sc) in next ch sp, cl] around, join in beg sc, turn. Fasten off.

Rnd 3: Working in sts on rnd 1 behind sts on rnd 2, join next color in any ch sp, ch 6 *(counts as first dc and ch-3)*, dc in same ch sp, *sc in next sc on rnd 2, dc in each of next 3 sts on rnd 1, sc in next sc on rnd 2**, (dc, ch 3, dc) in next ch sp on rnd 1, rep from * around, ending last rep at **, join in 3rd ch of beg ch-6, turn. Fasten off.

Rnd 4: Join next color with sc any corner ch sp, (cl, sc) in same ch sp, *cl, sk next 3 sts, sc in next st, cl**, (sc, cl, sc) in next ch sp, rep from * around, ending last rep at **, join in beg sc, turn. Fasten off.

Rnd 5: Working in sts on rnd 3 behind cl, join 2nd color in any corner ch sp, ch 6 *(counts as first dc and ch-3)*, dc in same ch sp, *[sc in next sc on rnd 4, dc in each of next 3 sts on rnd 3] twice**, sc in next sc on rnd 4, (dc, ch 3, dc) in next ch sp on rnd 3, rep from * around, ending last rep at **, join in 3rd ch of beg ch-6, turn. Fasten off.

Rnd 6: Join next color with sc any corner ch sp, (cl, sc) in same ch sp, *[cl, sk next 3 sts, sc in next st] twice, cl, sk next 3 sts**, (sc, cl, sc) in next ch sp, rep from * around, ending last rep at **, join in beg sc, turn. Fasten off.

Rnd 7: Working in sts on rnd 5 behind cl, join 2nd color in any corner ch sp, ch 6 *(counts as first dc and ch-3)*, dc in same ch sp, *[sc in next sc on rnd 6, dc in each of next 3 sts on rnd 5] 3 times**, sc in next sc on rnd 6, (dc, ch 3, dc) in next ch sp on rnd 5, rep from * around, ending last rep at **, join in 3rd ch of beg ch-6, **do not turn or fasten off.**

Rnd 8: Sl st in first ch sp, ch 3, (2 dc, ch 3, 3 dc) in same ch sp, *[ch 1, sk next 3 sts, 3 dc in next st] 3 times, ch 1, sk next 3 sts**, (3 dc, ch 3, 3 dc) in next corner ch sp, rep from * around, ending last rep at **, join in 3rd ch of beg ch-3. Fasten off. ∎

Square 25

FINISHED SIZE
9 inches square

GAUGE
Rnds 1–3 = 4 inches

PATTERN NOTES
Chain-3 at beginning of row or round counts as first double crochet unless otherwise stated.

Join with slip stitch as indicated unless otherwise stated.

Square is made with 4 colors with 1 of the colors a matching variegated.

INSTRUCTIONS
SQUARE
Rnd 1: With size H hook, ch 4, sl st in first ch to form ring, **ch 3** (*see Pattern Notes*), 2 dc in ring, ch 2, [3 dc in ring, ch 2] 3 times, **join** (*see Pattern Notes*) in 3rd ch of beg ch-3. Fasten off.

Rnd 2: Join next color with sc in any ch sp, ch 4, *sk next st, sc in next st, ch 4, sk next st**, sc in next ch sp, ch 4, rep from * around, ending last rep at **, join in beg sc.

Rnd 3: Sl st in first ch sp, ch 1, sc in same ch sp, ch 4, [sc in next ch sp, ch 4] around, join in beg sc. Fasten off.

Rnd 4: Join next color in any ch sp, ch 3, (2 dc, ch 3, 3 dc) in same ch sp (*corner*), *ch 1, 3 dc in next ch sp, ch 1**, (3 dc, ch 3, 3 dc) in next ch sp (*corner*), rep from * around, ending last rep at **, join in 3rd ch of beg ch-3. Fasten off.

Rnd 5: Join 2nd color with sc in any corner ch sp, ch 3, sc in same ch sp, *ch 3, [sc in next ch sp, ch 3] twice**, (sc, ch 3, sc) in next corner ch sp, rep from * around, ending last rep at **, join in beg sc.

Rnd 6: Sl st in first ch sp, ch 1, (sc, ch 3, sc) in same ch sp, ch 3, [sc in next ch sp, ch 3] 3 times**, (sc, ch 3, sc) in next ch sp, rep from * around, ending last rep at **, join in beg sc. Fasten off.

Rnd 7: Join next color in any corner ch sp, ch 3, (2 dc, ch 3, 3 dc) in same ch sp, *ch 1, [3 dc in next ch sp, ch 1] 4 times**, (3 dc, ch 3, 3 dc) in next corner ch sp, rep from * around, ending last rep at **, join in 3rd ch of beg ch-3. Fasten off.

Rnd 8: Join 2nd color with sc in any corner ch sp, ch 3, sc in same ch sp, *ch 3, [sc in next ch sp, ch 3] 5 times**, (sc, ch 3, sc) in next corner ch sp, rep from * around, ending last rep at **, join in beg sc.

Rnd 9: Sl st in first ch sp, ch 1, (sc, ch 3, sc) in same ch sp, ch 3, [sc in next ch sp, ch 3] 6 times**, (sc, ch 3, sc) in next ch sp, rep from * around, ending last rep at **, join in beg sc. Fasten off.

Rnd 10: Join first color in any corner ch sp, ch 3, (2 dc, ch 3, 3 dc) in same ch sp, *ch 1, [3 dc in next ch sp, ch 1] 7 times**, (3 dc, ch 3, 3 dc) in next corner ch sp, rep from * around, ending last rep at **, join in 3rd ch of beg ch-3. Fasten off.

Rnd 11: Join 2nd color with sc in any corner ch sp, ch 7, sc in same ch sp, *ch 5, [sc in next ch sp, ch 5] 8 times**, (sc, ch 7, sc) in next corner ch sp, rep from * around, ending last rep at **, join in beg sc. Fasten off. ■

Square 26

FINISHED SIZE
5½ inches

GAUGE
Rnds 1 & 2 = 2¾ inches

PATTERN NOTES
Chain-3 at beginning of row or round counts as first double crochet unless otherwise stated.

Join with slip stitch as indicated unless otherwise stated.

Square is made with 1 color and medium (worsted) weight yarn.

SPECIAL STITCHES
Beginning puff stitch (beg puff st): Ch 3 *(counts as first dc)*, [yo, insert hook in place indicated, yo, pull lp through] twice, yo, pull through all lps on hook.

Puff stitch (puff st): [Yo, insert hook in place indicated, yo, pull lp through] 3 times, yo, pull through all lps on hook.

INSTRUCTIONS
SQUARE
Rnd 1: With size H hook, ch 4, sl st in first ch to form ring, **ch 3** *(see Pattern Notes)*, 11 dc in ring, **join** *(see Pattern Notes)* in 3rd ch of beg ch-3.

Rnd 2: **Beg puff st** *(see Special Stitches)* in same st, *[ch 1, **puff st** *(see Special Stitches)* in next st] twice, ch 5 *(corner)* **, puff st in next st, rep from * around, ending last rep at **, join in beg puff st.

Rnd 3: Sl st in next ch sp, beg puff st in same ch sp, *ch 1, puff st in next ch sp, ch 2, 5 dc in next ch sp, ch 2**, puff st in next ch sp, rep from * around, ending last rep at **, join in beg puff st.

Rnd 4: Sl st in next ch sp, beg puff st in same ch sp, *ch 2, sk next st, [dc in next st, ch 1] twice, (dc, ch 1) 3 times in next st, dc in next st, ch 1, dc in next st, ch 2, sk next ch sp**, puff st in next ch sp, rep from * around, ending last rep at **, join in beg puff st.

Rnd 5: Ch 1, sc in each st and 2 in each ch sp around with 3 sc in center corner st, join in beg sc. Fasten off. ∎

Square 27

FINISHED SIZE

6 inches square

GAUGE

Rnds 1–3 = 4½ inches

PATTERN NOTES

Chain-3 at beginning of row or round counts as first double crochet unless otherwise stated.

Join with slip stitch as indicated unless otherwise stated.

Square is made with 2 colors of medium (worsted) weight yarn.

INSTRUCTIONS

SQUARE

Rnd 1: With size H hook, ch 6, sl st in first ch to form ring, **ch 3** *(see Pattern Notes)*, 2 dc in ring, ch 3, [3 dc in ring, ch 3] 3 times, **join** *(see Pattern Notes)* in 3rd ch of beg ch-3. Fasten off.

Rnd 2: Join next color in any ch sp, ch 3, (2 dc, ch 3, 3 dc) in same ch sp *(corner)*, *fpdc *(see Stitch Guide)* around each of next 3 sts**, (3 dc, ch 3, 3 dc) in next ch sp *(corner)*, rep from * around, ending last rep at **, join in 3rd ch of beg ch-3. Fasten off.

Rnd 3: Join first color in any corner ch sp, ch 3, (2 dc, ch 3, 3 dc) in same ch sp *(corner)*, *dc in each of next 3 sts, fpdc around each of next 3 fpdc, dc in each of next 3 sts**, (3 dc, ch 3, 3 dc) in next ch sp, rep from * around, ending last rep at **, join in 3rd ch of beg ch-3. Fasten off.

Rnd 4: Join 2nd color in any corner ch sp, ch 3, (2 dc, ch 3, 3 dc) in same ch sp *(corner)*, *dc in each of next 6 sts, fpdc around each of next 3 fpdc, dc in each of next 6 sts**, (3 dc, ch 3, 3 dc) in next ch sp, rep from * around, ending last rep at **, join in 3rd ch of beg ch-3. Fasten off. ■

Square 28

FINISHED SIZE

4½ inches square

GAUGE

Rnds 1 & 2 = 3 inches

PATTERN NOTES

Chain-3 at beginning of row or round counts as first double crochet unless otherwise stated.

Join with slip stitch as indicated unless otherwise stated.

Square is made with 1 color of medium (worsted) weight yarn.

SPECIAL STITCHES

Beginning popcorn (beg pc): Ch 3 *(counts as first dc)*, 4 dc in ring, drop lp from hook, insert hook in 3rd ch of beg ch-3, pull dropped lp through, ch 1 to secure.

Popcorn (pc): 5 dc in place indicated, drop lp from hook, insert hook in first dc of group, pull dropped lp through, ch 1 to secure.

INSTRUCTIONS

SQUARE

Rnd 1: With size H hook, ch 4, sl st in first ch to form ring, **beg pc** *(see Special Stitches)* in ring, ch 3, [**pc** (*see Special Stitches*) in ring, ch 3] 7 times, **join** (*see Pattern Notes*) in beg pc.

Rnd 2: Sl st in first ch sp, **ch 3** (*see Pattern Notes*), (2 dc, ch 3, 3 dc) in same ch sp, *2 dc in next ch sp**, (3 dc, ch 3, 3 dc) in next ch sp, rep from * around, ending last rep at **, join in 3rd ch of beg ch-3.

Rnd 3: Ch 1, sc in first st, sc in each of next 2 sts, (3 dc, ch 3, sl st in 3rd ch from hook, 3 dc) in next ch sp, *sc in each of next 8 sts**, (3 dc, ch 3, sl st in 3rd ch from hook, 3 dc) in next ch sp, rep from * around, ending last rep at **, join in beg sc. Fasten off. ■

Square 29

FINISHED SIZE
4½ inches square

GAUGE
Rnds 1 & 2 = 3½ inches

PATTERN NOTES
Join with slip stitch as indicated unless otherwise stated.

Square is made with 2 colors of medium (worsted) weight yarn.

INSTRUCTIONS
SQUARE
Rnd 1: With size H hook, ch 4, sl st in first ch to form ring, [sc in ring, ch 3, 4 dc in ring, ch 3] 4 times, **join** (*see Pattern Notes*) in beg sc.

Rnd 2: Sl st in each of first 2 chs of next ch-3, sc in next ch, *ch 3, **dc dec** (*see Stitch Guide*) in next 4 sts, ch 3, sc in next ch, ch 2**, sc in 3rd ch of next ch-3, rep from * around, ending last rep at **, join in beg sc. Fasten off.

Rnd 3: Join next color with sc in any dc dec, *ch 4, working over ch 2 of last rnd, (dc, ch 2, dc) in ring on rnd 1, ch 4**, sc in next dc dec, rep from * around, ending last rep at **, join in beg sc.

Rnd 4: Ch 1, sc in first st, *2 sc in next ch-4 sp, (4 dc, ch 3, sl st in 3rd ch from hook, 4 dc) in next ch-2 sp, 2 sc in next ch-4 sp**, sc in next st, rep from * around, ending last rep at **, join in beg sc. Fasten off. ■

Square 30

FINISHED SIZE
5¼ inches square

GAUGE
Rnds 1–4 = 4 inches

PATTERN NOTES

Chain-3 at beginning of row or round counts as first double crochet unless otherwise stated.

Join with slip stitch as indicated unless otherwise stated.

Square is made with 3 colors of medium (worsted) weight yarn.

INSTRUCTIONS
SQUARE

Rnd 1: With size H hook, ch 4, sl st in first ch to form ring, ch 1, [sc in ring, ch 3] 4 times, **join** *(see Pattern Notes)* in beg sc.

Rnd 2: Sl st in first ch sp, **ch 3** *(see Pattern Notes)*, (2 dc, ch 3, 3 dc) in same ch sp *(corner)*, (3 dc, ch 3, 3 dc) in each ch sp around, join in 3rd ch of beg ch-3. Fasten off.

Rnd 3: Join next color with sc in any ch sp, ch 3, sc in same ch sp *(corner)*, *ch 3, sk next 3 sts, sc in sp between dc groups, ch 3**, (sc, ch 3, sc) in next ch sp *(corner)*, rep from * around, ending last rep at **, join in beg sc.

Rnd 4: Sl st in first ch sp, ch 3, (2 dc, ch 3, 3 dc) in same ch sp, 3 dc in each of next 2 ch sps**, (3 dc, ch 3, 3 dc) in next corner ch sp, rep from * around, ending last rep at **, join in 3rd ch of beg ch-3. Fasten off.

Rnd 5: Join next color with sc in any corner ch sp, ch 3, sc in same ch sp, *[ch 3, sk next 3 dc, sc in sp between dc groups] 3 times, ch 3**, (sc, ch 3, sc) in next corner ch sp, rep from * around, ending last rep at **, join in beg sc.

Rnd 6: Sl st in first ch sp, ch 3, (2 dc, ch 3, 3 dc) in same ch sp, *3 dc in each of next 4 ch sps**, (3 dc, ch 3, 3 dc) in next ch sp, rep from * around, join in 3rd ch of beg ch-3. Fasten off. ∎

Square 31

FINISHED SIZE
5½ inches

GAUGE
Rnds 1 & 2 = 3 inches

PATTERN NOTES

Chain-3 at beginning of row or round counts as first double crochet unless otherwise stated.

Join with slip stitch as indicated unless otherwise stated.

Square is made with 2 colors of medium (worsted) weight yarn.

INSTRUCTIONS
SQUARE

Rnd 1: With size H hook, ch 6, sl st in first ch to form ring, ch 1, 18 sc in ring, **join** *(see Pattern Notes)* in beg sc. Fasten off.

Rnd 2: Join next color in first st, [ch 5, **tr dec** *(see Stitch Guide)* in next 3 sts, ch 5, sl st in same st as last tr] 5 times, ch 5, tr dec in next 2 sts and same st as first sl st, ch 5, join in beg sl st. Fasten off.

Rnd 3: Join first color with sc in top of any tr dec, ch 6 [sc in top of next tr dec, ch 6] around, join in beg sc.

Rnd 4: Sl st in first ch sp, ch 1, 8 sc in this ch sp and in each ch sp around, join in beg sc. Fasten off.

Rnd 5: Join 2nd color in first st, **ch 3** *(see Pattern Notes)*, (dc, ch 1, 2 dc) in same st *(corner)*, *[ch 1, sk next st, dc in next st] 5 times, ch 1, sk next st**, (2 dc, ch 1, 2 dc) in next st *(corner)*, rep from * around, ending last rep at **, join in 3rd ch of next ch-3. Fasten off.

Rnd 6: Join first color in any corner ch sp, ch 3, (dc, ch 1, 2 dc) in same ch sp, *ch 1, dc in sp between next 2 sts, [ch 1, dc in next ch sp] 6 times, ch 1, sc in sp between next 2 sts, ch 1**, (2 dc, ch 1, 2 dc) in next corner ch sp, rep from * around, ending last rep at **, join in 3rd ch of beg ch-3. Fasten off. ∎

Square **32**

FINISHED SIZE
5¾ inches

GAUGE
Rnds 1 & 2 = 2¾ inches

PATTERN NOTES
Chain-3 at beginning of row or round counts as first double crochet unless otherwise stated.

Join with slip stitch as indicated unless otherwise stated.

Square is made with 2 colors of medium (worsted) weight yarn.

INSTRUCTIONS
SQUARE
Rnd 1: With size H hook, ch 6, sl st in first ch to form ring, **ch 3** *(see Pattern Notes)*, 23 dc in ring, **join** *(see Pattern Notes)* in 3rd ch of beg ch-3.

Rnd 2: Ch 1, sc in each of first 3 sts, ch 6, sk next 3 sts, [sc in each of next 3 sts, ch 6, sk next 3 sts] around, join in beg sc. Fasten off.

Rnd 3: Join next color in any ch sp, ch 4 *(counts as first tr)*, 11 tr in same ch sp, ch 4, [12 tr in next ch sp, ch 4] around, join in 4th ch of beg ch-4. Fasten off.

Rnd 4: Join first color in any ch sp, ch 4, 8 tr in same ch sp, *ch 3, sk next 4 sts, sc in next st, ch 3, sk next 2 sts, sc in next st, ch 3**, 9 tr in next ch sp, rep from * around, ending last rep at **, join in 4th ch of beg ch-4. Fasten off. ∎

Square **33**

FINISHED SIZE
4½ inches square

GAUGE
Rnds 1 & 2 = 2½ inches

PATTERN NOTES
Join with slip stitch as indicated unless otherwise stated.

Square is made with 2 colors of medium (worsted) weight yarn.

SPECIAL STITCHES
Beginning puff stitch (beg puff st): Ch 3, [yo, insert hook in place indicated, yo, pull lp through] twice, yo, pull through all lps on hook.

Puff stitch (puff st): [Yo, insert hook in place indicated, yo, pull lp through] 3 times, yo, pull through all lps on hook.

INSTRUCTIONS
SQUARE
Rnd 1: With size H hook, ch 6, sl st in first ch to form ring, ch 1, 16 sc in ring, **join** *(see Pattern Notes)* in beg sc. Fasten off.

Rnd 2: Join next color in any st, ch 4 *(counts as first dc and ch-1)*, [dc in next st, ch 1] around, join in 3rd ch of beg ch-4. Fasten off.

Rnd 3: Join first color in any ch sp, **beg puff st** *(see Special Stitches)* in same ch sp, ch 3, [**puff st** *(see Special Stitches)* in next ch sp, ch 3] around, join in beg puff st. Fasten off.

Rnd 4: Join 2nd color in any ch sp, ch 3 *(counts as first dc)*, (2 dc, ch 5, sl st in 3rd ch from hook, ch 2, 3 dc) in same ch sp, *ch 2, [sc in next ch sp, ch 3] twice, sc in next ch sp, ch 2**, (3 dc, ch 5, sl st in 3rd ch from hook, ch 2, 3 dc) in next ch sp, rep from * around, ending last rep at **, join in 3rd ch of beg ch-3. Fasten off. ■

Square 34

FINISHED SIZE
6 inches square

GAUGE
Rnds 1 & 2 = 2¼ inches

PATTERN NOTES
Join with slip stitch as indicated unless otherwise stated.

Square is made with 2 colors of medium (worsted) weight yarn.

INSTRUCTIONS
SQUARE
Rnd 1: With size H hook, ch 6, sl st in first ch to form ring, ch 1, 16 sc in ring, **join** *(see Pattern Notes)* in beg sc.

Rnd 2: Ch 6 *(counts as first dc and ch-3)*, dc in same st *(corner)*, *ch 1, sk next st, dc in next st, ch 1, sk next st**, (dc, ch 3, dc) in next st *(corner)*, rep from * around, ending last rep at **, join in 3rd ch of beg ch-6. Fasten off.

Rnd 3: Join next color with sc in any corner ch sp, 4 sc in same ch sp, *[sc in next st, working behind ch sps, dc in sk st on rnd 1] twice, sc in next st**, 5 sc in next corner ch sp, rep from * around, ending last rep at **, join in beg sc.

Rnd 4: Ch 4 *(counts as first dc and ch-1)*, *sk next st, (dc, ch 3, dc) in next st**, [ch 1, sk next st, dc in next st] 4 times, ch 1, rep from * around, ending last rep at **, [ch 1, sk next st, dc in next st] 3 times, ch 1, join in 3rd ch of beg ch-4. Fasten off.

Rnd 5: Join first color with sc in any corner ch sp, 4 sc in same ch sp, *[sc in next st, working behind ch sps, dc in sk sp on rnd 3] 5 times, sc in next st**, 5 sc in next corner ch sp, rep from * around, ending last rep at **, join in beg sc.

Rnd 6: Ch 4 *(counts as first dc and ch-1)*, *sk next st, (dc, ch 3, dc) in next st**, [ch 1, sk next st, dc in next st] 7 times, ch 1, rep from * around, ending last rep at **, [ch 1, sk next st, dc in next st] 5 times, ch 1, sk next st, join in 3rd ch of beg ch-4. Fasten off.

Rnd 7: Join with sc in any corner ch sp, 4 sc in same ch sp, *[sc in next st, working behind ch sps, dc in sk st on rnd 5] 8 times, sc in next st**, 5 sc in next corner ch sp, rep from * around, ending last rep at **, join in beg sc. Fasten off. ∎

Square 35

FINISHED SIZE
5¼ inches square

GAUGE
Rnds 1 & 2 = 3¼ inches

PATTERN NOTES
Chain-5 at beginning of row or round counts as first double crochet and chain-2 unless otherwise stated.

Join with slip stitch as indicated unless otherwise stated.

Square is made with 1 color of medium (worsted) weight yarn.

SPECIAL STITCHES
Beginning popcorn (beg pc): Ch 3 *(counts as first dc)*, 3 dc in place indicated, drop lp from hook, insert hook in 3rd ch of beg ch-3, pull dropped lp through, ch 1 to secure.

Popcorn (pc): 4 dc in place indicated, drop lp from hook, insert hook in first dc of group, pull dropped lp through, ch 1 to secure.

INSTRUCTIONS
SQUARE
Rnd 1: Ch 8, sl st in first ch to form ring, **beg pc** *(see Special Stitches)* in ring, *ch 1, **pc** *(see Special Stitches)* in ring, ch 3, (pc, ch 1, pc) in ring, ch 3*, pc in ring, rep between * once, **join** *(see Pattern Notes)* in beg pc.

Rnd 2: Ch 5 *(see Pattern Notes)*, dc in next pc, *ch 2, (pc, ch 3, pc) in next ch-3 sp *(corner)***, [ch 2, dc in next pc] twice, rep from * around, ending last rep at **, ch 2, join in 3rd ch of beg ch-5.

Rnd 3: Ch 5, sk next ch sp, dc in next st, ch 2, sk next ch sp, dc in next st, *ch 2, (pc, ch 3, pc) in next corner ch sp, ch 2**, [dc in next st, ch 2, sk next ch sp] 4 times, rep from * around, ending last rep at **, dc in next st, ch 2, join in 3rd ch of beg ch-5.

Rnd 4: Ch 5, sk next ch sp, [dc in next st, ch 2, sk next ch sp] twice, dc in next st, *ch 2, (pc, ch 3, pc) in next corner ch sp, ch 2**, [dc in next st, ch 2, sk next ch sp] 6 times, rep from * around, ending last rep at **, dc in next st, ch 2, sk next ch sp, dc in next st, ch 2, sk next ch sp, join in 3rd ch of beg ch-5. Fasten off. ∎

Square 36

FINISHED SIZE
7½ inches square

GAUGE
Rnds 1–3 = 4 inches

PATTERN NOTES
Chain-3 at beginning of row or round counts as first double crochet unless otherwise stated.

Join with slip stitch as indicated unless otherwise stated.

Square in made with 1 color of medium (worsted) weight yarn.

SPECIAL STITCHES
Beginning popcorn (beg pc): Ch 3 (*counts as first dc*), 3 dc in place indicated, drop lp from hook, insert hook in 3rd ch of beg ch-3, pull dropped lp through, ch 1 to secure.

Popcorn (pc): 4 dc in place indicated, drop lp from hook, insert hook in first dc of group, pull dropped lp through, ch 1 to secure.

INSTRUCTIONS
SQUARE
Rnd 1: With size H hook, ch 8, sl st in first ch to form ring, **ch 3** (*see Pattern Notes*), 15 dc in ring, **join** (*see Pattern Notes*) in 3rd ch of beg ch-3. (*16 dc*)

Rnd 2: Ch 4 (*counts as first dc and ch-1*), [dc in next st, ch 1] around, join in 3rd ch of beg ch-4.

Rnd 3: Sl st in first ch sp, **beg pc** (*see Special Stitches*) in same ch sp, ch 2, [**pc** (*see Special Stitches*) in next ch sp, ch 2] around, join in beg pc.

Rnd 4: Sl st in next ch sp, ch 3, (dc, ch 3, 2 dc) in same ch sp (*corner*), *[ch 3, sc in next ch sp] 3 times, ch 3**, (2 dc, ch 3, 2 dc) in next ch sp (*corner*), rep from * around, ending last rep at **, join in 3rd ch of beg ch-3.

Rnd 5: Sl st in next st and in next ch sp, ch 3, (2 dc, ch 3, 3 dc) in next ch sp (*corner*), *[ch 2, 3 dc in next ch sp] 4 times, ch 2**, (3 dc, ch 3, 3 dc) in next corner ch sp, rep from * around, ending last rep at **, join in 3rd ch of beg ch-3.

Rnd 6: Sl st in each of next 2 sts and in next ch sp, (beg pc, ch 3, pc) in same ch sp, *[ch 2, pc in next ch sp] 5 times, ch 2**, (pc, ch 3, pc) in next ch sp, rep from * around, ending last rep at **, join in beg pc. Fasten off. ∎

Square 37

FINISHED SIZE
4 inches square

GAUGE
Rnd 1 = 2 inches in diameter

PATTERN NOTES
Chain-3 at beginning of round counts as first double crochet unless otherwise stated.

Join with slip stitch as indicated unless otherwise stated.

Square is made with 1 color of medium (worsted) weight yarn.

SPECIAL STITCHES
Beginning cluster (beg cl): Ch 3 (*counts as first dc*), holding back last lp of each st on hook, 3 dc in place indicated, yo, pull through all lps on hook.

Cluster (cl): Holding back last lp of each st on hook, 4 dc in place indicated, yo, pull through all lps on hook.

INSTRUCTIONS
SQUARE
Rnd 1: With size H hook, ch 6, sl st in first ch to form ring, **ch 3** (*see Pattern Notes*), 2 dc in ring,

[ch 2, 3 dc in ring] 3 times, join with hdc in 3rd ch of beg ch-3 forming last ch sp.

Rnd 2: Beg cl (*see Special Stitches*) in ch sp just made, [ch 3, (**cl**—*see Special Stitches*, ch 5, cl) in next ch sp] around, ch 3, cl in same ch sp as beg cl, ch 2, join with dc in top of beg cl forming last ch sp.

Rnd 3: Ch 3, 3 dc in same ch sp, *2 **fptr** (*see Stitch Guide*) around 3 dc at same time on rnd 1**, (4 dc, ch 3, 4 dc) in next ch sp, rep from * around, ending last rep at **, 4 dc in same ch sp as beg ch-3, ch 3, **join** (*see Pattern Notes*) in 3rd ch of beg ch-3. Fasten off. ∎

Square 38

FINISHED SIZE
6½ inches

GAUGE
Rnds 1 & 2 = 3 inches

PATTERN NOTES
Chain-3 at beginning of row or round counts as first double crochet unless otherwise stated.

Join with slip stitch as indicated unless otherwise stated.

Square is made with 2 colors of medium (worsted) weight yarn.

INSTRUCTIONS
SQUARE

Rnd 1: With size H hook, ch 6, sl st in first ch to form ring, **ch 3** *(see Pattern Notes)*, 2 dc in ring, ch 3, [3 dc in ring, ch 3] 3 times, **join** *(see Pattern Notes)* in 3rd ch of beg ch-3. Fasten off.

Rnd 2: Join next color in any ch sp, ch 3, (2 dc, ch 3, 3 dc) in same ch sp *(corner)*, ch 2, [(3 dc, ch 3, 3 dc) in next ch sp *(corner)*, ch 2] around, join in 3rd ch of beg ch-3. Fasten off.

Rnd 3: Join first color in any corner ch sp, ch 3, (2 dc, ch 3, 3 dc) in same ch sp, *dc in each of next 3 sts, 2 dc in next ch sp, dc in each of next 3 sts**, (3 dc, ch 3, 3 dc) in next corner ch sp, rep from * around, ending last rep at **, join in 3rd ch of beg ch-3. Fasten off.

Rnd 4: Join 2nd color in any corner ch sp, ch 3, (2 dc, ch 1, 3 dc) in same ch sp, *[sk next 2 sts, 3 dc in next st] 4 times, sk next 2 sts**, (3 dc, ch 1, 3 dc) in next corner ch sp, rep from * around, ending last rep at **, join in 3rd ch of beg ch-3. Fasten off.

Rnd 5: Join first color in any corner ch sp, ch 3, (2 dc, ch 1, 3 dc) in same ch sp, dc in each st around with (3 dc, ch 1, 3 dc) in each corner ch sp, join in 3rd ch of beg ch-3. Fasten off. ■

Square 39

FINISHED SIZE
5 inches square

GAUGE
Rnds 1 & 2 = 3 inches

PATTERN NOTES
Chain-3 at beginning of row or round counts as first double crochet unless otherwise stated.

Join with slip stitch as indicated unless otherwise stated.

Square is made with 1 color of medium (worsted) weight yarn.

INSTRUCTIONS
SQUARE

Rnd 1: With size H hook, ch 8, sl st in first ch to form ring, **ch 3** *(see Pattern Notes)*, dc in ring, ch 6, [2 dc in ring, ch 6] 3 times, **join** *(see Pattern Notes)* in 3rd ch of beg ch-3.

Rnd 2: Ch 1, sc in first st, *sc in next st, (hdc, 2 dc, 3 tr, 2 dc, hdc) in next ch sp *(corner)***, sc in next st, rep from * around, ending last rep at **, join in beg sc.

Rnd 3: Sl st in sp between first and 2nd sts, ch 9 *(counts as first dc and ch-6)*, *sc in center tr of next corner group, ch 6**, dc in sp between next 2 sc, ch 6, rep from * around, ending last rep at **, join in 3rd ch of beg ch-9.

Rnd 4: Ch 1, 6 sc in first ch sp, *(4 dc, ch 6, sl st in top of last st, 4 dc) in next sc, 6 sc in next ch sp, ch 6, sl st in top of last st**, 6 sc in next ch sp, rep from * around, ending last rep at **, join in beg sc. Fasten off. ■

Square 40

FINISHED SIZE
6¾ inches square

GAUGE
2 dc rows = 1½ inches

PATTERN NOTES
Chain-5 at beginning of row or round counts as first double crochet and ch-2 unless otherwise stated.

Chain-3 at beginning of row or round counts as first double crochet unless otherwise stated.

Join with slip stitch as indicated unless otherwise stated.

Square is made with 1 color of medium (worsted) weight yarn.

INSTRUCTIONS
SQUARE
Row 1: With size H hook, ch 20, dc in 8th ch from hook (*first chs counts as 2 sk chs, first dc and ch-2*), [ch 2, sk next 2 chs, dc in next ch] across, turn. (*5 ch sps, 6 dc*)

Rows 2–5: Ch 5 (*see Pattern Notes*), sk next ch sp, dc in next st, [ch 2, sk next ch sp, dc in next st] across, turn. At end of last rnd, fasten off.

Rnd 6: Now working in rnds around outer edge, working in ends of rows and across starting ch on opposite side of row 1, **join** (*see Pattern Notes*) in any corner, **ch 3** (*see Pattern Notes*), 9 dc in same corner, *2 dc in each of next 3 ch sps**, 10 dc in next corner, rep from * around, ending last rep at ** join in 3rd ch of beg ch-3.

Rnd 7: Ch 1, sc in first st, *ch 4, sc between 6th and 7th dc of this dc group, ch 4, sc in last st of this group, ch 6, sk next 6 sts**, sc in first st of next dc group, rep from * around, ending last rep at **, join in beg sc. Fasten off.

Rnd 8: Join in any ch-6 sp, ch 3, (5 dc, ch 3, 6 dc) in same ch sp (*corner*), *ch 5, sk next ch sp, sc in next sc, ch 5, sk next ch sp**, (6 dc, ch 3, 6 dc) in next ch-6 sp (*corner*), rep from * around, ending last rep at **, join in 3rd ch of beg ch-3. Fasten off. ∎

Square 41

FINISHED SIZE
6 inches square

GAUGE
Rnds 1 & 2 = 3½ inches

PATTERN NOTES
Join with slip stitch as indicated unless otherwise stated.

Square is made with 1 color of medium (worsted) weight yarn.

INSTRUCTIONS
SQUARE

Rnd 1: With size H hook, ch 6, sl st in first ch to form ring, ch 4 *(counts as first dc and ch-1)*, [dc in ring, ch 1] 11 times, **join** *(see Pattern Notes)* in 3rd ch of beg ch-4.

Rnd 2: Sl st in first ch sp, ch 4 *(counts as first tr)*, tr in same ch sp, ch 1, [2 tr in next ch sp, ch 1] around, join in 4th ch of beg ch-5.

Rnd 3: Sl st in next st, ch 1, sc in first ch sp, *ch 10, sc in next ch sp**, [ch 5, sc in next ch sp] twice, rep from * around, ending last rep at **, ch 5, sc in next ch sp, ch 5, join in beg sc.

Rnd 4: Sl st in first ch sp, ch 3 *(counts as first dc)*, 13 dc in same ch sp, *(3 sc, ch 3, sl st in 3rd ch from hook, 3 sc) in each of next 2 ch sps**, 14 dc in next ch sp, rep from * around, ending last rep at **, join in 3rd ch of beg ch-3. Fasten off. ∎

Square 42

FINISHED SIZE
6 inches

GAUGE
Rnd 1 = 2 inches in diameter

PATTERN NOTES
Chain-3 at beginning of row or round counts as first double crochet unless otherwise stated.

Join with slip stitch as indicated unless otherwise stated.

Square is made with 4 colors of medium (worsted) weight yarn.

INSTRUCTIONS
SQUARE

Rnd 1: With size H hook, ch 6, sl st in first ch to form ring, **ch 3** *(see Pattern Notes)*, 15 dc in ring, **join** *(see Pattern Notes)* in 3rd ch of beg ch-3.

Rnd 2: Ch 1, sc in first st, ch 5, sk next st, [sc in next st, ch 5, sk next st] around, join in beg sc. Fasten off.

Rnd 3: Join next color in any ch sp, ch 2 *(counts as first hdc)*, (hdc, 4 dc, ch 3, sl st in last st, 4 dc, 2 hdc) in same ch sp, (2 hdc, 4 dc, ch 3, sl st in last st, 4 dc, 2 hdc) in each ch sp around, join in 2nd ch of beg ch-2. Fasten off.

Rnd 4: Working behind last rnd around sc on rnd 2, join next color with **bpsc** *(see Stitch Guide)* around any sc on rnd 2, ch 5, [bpsc around next sc on rnd 2, ch 5] around, join in beg bpsc.

Rnd 5: Sl st in first ch sp, ch 3, 6 dc in same ch sp, *(3 dc, ch 3, 3 dc) in next ch sp *(corner)**, 7 dc in next ch sp, rep from * around, ending last rep at **, join in 3rd ch of beg ch-3.

Rnd 6: Ch 3, dc in each st around, with (dc, ch 3, dc) in each corner ch sp, join in 3rd ch of beg ch-3. Fasten off.

Rnd 7: Join next color in any corner ch sp, ch 4 *(counts as first tr)*, (tr, ch 3, 2 tr) in same ch sp, *sk next st, [3 **fpdc** *(see Stitch Guide)* around next st, sk next 2 sts] 4 times, 3 fpdc around next st, sk next st**, (2 tr, ch 3, 2 tr) in corner ch sp, rep from * around, ending last rep at **, join in 4th ch of beg ch-4. Fasten off. ∎

Square 43

FINISHED SIZE
5½ inches square

GAUGE
Rnd 1 = 1 inch in diameter

PATTERN NOTES
Join with slip stitch as indicated unless otherwise stated.

Square is made with 3 colors of medium (worsted) weight yarn.

SPECIAL STITCHES
Beginning cluster (beg cl): Ch 3 *(counts as first dc)*, holding back last lp of each st on hook, 2 dc in place indicated, yo, pull through all lps on hook.

Cluster (cl): Holding back last lp of each st on hook, 3 dc in place indicated, yo, pull through all lps on hook.

INSTRUCTIONS
SQUARE
Rnd 1: With size H hook, ch 2, 8 sc in 2nd ch from hook, **join** *(see Pattern Notes)* in beg sc. Fasten off.

Rnd 2: Join next color in first st, ch 9, [sl st in next st, ch 9] around, join in beg sl st.

Rnd 3: Working behind ch-9 sps, ch 3, [sl st in next st, ch 3] around, join in joining sl st of last rnd,

Rnd 4: Sl st in first ch sp, *(ch 9, sl st) 3 times in same ch sp, *sl st in next st**, sl st in next ch sp, rep from * around, ending last rep at **, join in beg sl st.

Rnd 5: Working behind ch-9 sps, ch 3, [sl st in next st between groups of ch-9 sps, ch 3] around, join in joining sl st of last rnd,

Rnd 6: Sl st in first ch sp, *(ch 9, sl st) 3 times in same ch sp, *sl st in next st**, sl st in next ch sp, rep from * around, ending last rep at **, join in beg sl st.

Rnd 7: Working behind ch-9 sps, ch 4, [sl st in next st between ch-9 sps, ch 4] around, join in joining sl st of last rnd. Fasten off.

Rnd 8: Join next color in any ch sp, (**beg cl**—*see Special Stitches*, ch 5, **cl**—*see Special Stitches*) in same ch sp *(corner)*, *ch 2, 3 dc in next ch sp, ch 3**, (cl, ch 5, cl) in next ch sp *(corner)*, rep from * around, ending last rep at **, join in beg cl.

Rnd 9: Sl st in first corner ch sp, (beg cl, ch 4, cl) in same ch sp, *[ch 2, 3 dc in next ch sp] twice, ch 2**, (cl, ch 4, cl) in next corner ch sp, rep from * around, ending last rep at **, join in beg cl. Fasten off. ∎

Square 44

FINISHED SIZE
5 inches square

GAUGE
Rnds 1 & 2 = 3 inches

PATTERN NOTES
Chain-3 at beginning of round counts as first double crochet unless otherwise stated.

Join with slip stitch as indicated unless otherwise stated.

Square is made with 3 colors of medium (worsted) weight yarn.

INSTRUCTIONS
SQUARE
Rnd 1: With size H hook, ch 6, sl st in first ch to form ring, ch 1, 16 sc in ring, **join** (see Pattern Notes) in beg sc.

Rnd 2: Ch 1, sc in first st, *(sl st, ch 3, dc, ch 3, sl st) in next st**, sc in next st, rep from * around, ending last rep at **, join in beg sc. Fasten off.

Rnd 3: Join next color with sc in any dc, *3 dc in next sc**, sc in next dc, rep from * around, ending last rep at **, join in beg sc.

Rnd 4: Ch 3 (see Pattern Notes), (2 dc, ch 2, 3 dc) in same st (corner), *ch 1, 3 dc in next sc, ch 1**, (3 dc, ch 2, 3 dc) in next sc (corner), rep from * around, ending last rep at **, join in 3rd ch of beg ch-3. Fasten off.

Rnd 5: Join next color in any corner ch sp, ch 3, (2 dc, ch 2, 3 dc) in same ch sp (corner), *ch 1, [3 dc in next ch sp, ch 1] twice**, (3 dc, ch 2, 3 dc) in next corner ch sp (corner), rep from * around, ending last rep at **, join in 3rd ch of beg ch-3. Fasten off.

Rnd 6: Join first color with sc in any corner ch sp, 2 sc in same ch sp, sc in each st and in each ch-1 sp around with 3 sc in each corner ch sp, join in beg sc. Fasten off. ■

Square 45

FINISHED SIZE
7½ inches square

GAUGE
Rnd 1 = 1½ inches in diameter

PATTERN NOTES
Join with slip stitch as indicated unless otherwise stated.

Square is made with 3 colors of medium (worsted) weight yarn.

INSTRUCTIONS
SQUARE

Rnd 1: With size H hook, ch 4, 7 dc in 4th ch from hook (*first 3 chs count as first dc*), **join** (*see Pattern Notes*) in 3rd ch of beg ch-3.

Rnd 2: Ch 6 (*counts as first dc and ch-3*), [dc in next st, ch 3] around, join in 3rd ch of beg ch-6.

Rnd 3: Ch 1, (sc, hdc, 3 dc, hdc, sc) in each ch-3 sp around, join in beg sc. Fasten off. (*8 petals*)

Rnd 4: Working behind sts on last rnd, join next color with **fpsc** (*see Stitch Guide*) around any dc on rnd 2, ch 5, [fpsc around next dc on rnd 2, ch 5] around, join in beg fpsc.

Rnd 5: Ch 1, (sc, hdc, dc, 5 tr, dc, hdc, sc) in each ch sp around, join in beg sc. Fasten off. (*8 petals*)

Rnd 6: Working behind petals, join next color with fpsc around fpsc on rnd 4, ch 6, [fpsc around fpsc on rnd 4, ch 6] around, join in beg fpsc.

Rnd 7: Ch 1, (sc, hdc, dc, 6 tr, dc, hdc, sc) in each ch sp around, join in beg sc. (*8 petals*)

Rnd 8: Ch 6 (*counts as dtr and ch-1*), *sk next 3 sts, dc in each of next 4 tr, ch 1, sk next 3 sts, dtr in last st on this group, dtr in first sc of next group, sk next 3 sts, dc in each of next 4 tr, ch 1, sk next 3 sts, dtr in last sc of this group, ch 3 (*corner*)**, dtr in first sc of next group, ch 1, rep from * around, ending last rep at **, join in 5th ch of beg ch-6.

Rnd 9: Ch 1, hdc in first st, hdc in each st and in each ch-1 sp around with (3 dc, ch 3, 3 dc) in each corner ch sp, join in beg hdc. Fasten off. ■

Square 46

FINISHED SIZE
8½ inches square

GAUGE
Rnd 1 = 2½ inches in diameter

PATTERN NOTES
Chain-3 at beginning of row or round counts as first double crochet unless otherwise stated.

Join with slip stitch as indicated unless otherwise stated.

Square is made with 3 colors of medium (worsted) weight yarn.

SPECIAL STITCHES
Beginning cluster (beg cl): Ch 3 (*counts as first dc*), holding back last lp of each st on hook, 2 dc in place indicated, yo, pull through all lps on hook.

Cluster (cl): Holding back last lp of each st on hook, 3 dc in place indicated, yo, pull through all lps on hook.

INSTRUCTIONS
SQUARE

Rnd 1: With size H hook, ch 6, sl st in first ch to form ring, **beg cl** *(see Special Stitches)* in ring, ch 3, [**cl** *(see Special Stitches)* in ring, ch 3] 7 times, **join** *(see Pattern Notes)* in beg cl. Fasten off.

Rnd 2: Join next color in any ch sp, **ch 3** *(see Pattern Notes)*, 5 dc in same ch sp, 6 dc in each ch sp around, join in 3rd ch of beg ch-3. Fasten off.

Rnd 3: Join next color with sc in first st, *ch 3, sk next st, sc in next st, ch 6, sc in 2nd ch from hook, hdc in next ch, dc in next ch, tr in next ch, dtr in next ch *(petal)*, sk next 3 sts**, sc in next st, rep from * around, ending last rep at **, join in beg sc. Fasten off. *(8 petals)*

Rnd 4: Join first color in any ch sp, ch 4 *(counts as first tr)*, 2 tr in same ch sp, *ch 3, sc in top of next petal, ch 3**, 3 tr in next ch sp, rep from * around, ending last rep at **, join in 4th ch of beg ch-4.

Rnd 5: Join 2nd color in any sc, ch 3, (2 dc, ch 3, 3 dc) in same st *(corner)*, *sc in next ch sp, ch 5, 2 sc in next ch sp, sc in next st, 2 sc in next ch sp, ch 5, sc in next ch sp**, (3 dc, ch 3, 3 dc) in next sc *(corner)*, rep from * around, ending last rep at **, join in 3rd ch of beg ch-3.

Rnd 6: Ch 3, hdc in each of next 2 sts, *5 sc in next corner ch sp, hdc in each of next 2 sts, dc in each of next 2 sts, (hdc, 3 sc) in next ch sp, sc in each of next 5 sts, (3 sc, hdc) in next ch sp, dc in each of next 2 sts, hdc in each of next 2 sts*, rep from * around, ending last rep at **, dc in last st, join in 3rd ch of beg ch-3.

Rnd 7: Ch 1, sc in first st and in each st around with 3 sc in each center corner st, join in beg sc. Fasten off. ∎

Square 47

FINISHED SIZE
6 inches square

GAUGE
Rnds 1 & 2 = 3 inches

PATTERN NOTES
Chain-3 at beginning of row or round counts as first double crochet unless otherwise stated.

Join with slip stitch as indicated unless otherwise stated.

Square is made with 3 colors of medium (worsted) weight yarn.

SPECIAL STITCH
Popcorn (pc): 5 dc in place indicated, drop lp from hook, insert hook in first dc of group, pull dropped lp through, ch 1 to secure.

INSTRUCTIONS
SQUARE

Rnd 1: Ch 6, sl st in first ch to form ring, ch 1, sc in ring, *ch 3, **pc** *(see Special Stitch)* in ring, ch 3**, sc in ring, rep from * around, ending last rep at **, **join** *(see Pattern Notes)* in beg sc.

Rnd 2: Ch 1, sc in first st, ch 7, [sc in next sc, ch 7] around, join in beg sc.

Rnd 3: Ch 1, sc in first st, *ch 5, pc in next ch sp, ch 5**, sc in next st, rep from * around, ending last rep at **, join in beg sc. Fasten off.

Rnd 4: Join next color in any pc, **ch 3** *(see Pattern Notes)*, (2 dc, ch 2, 3 dc) in same st *(corner)*, *[ch 1, 3 dc in next ch sp] twice, ch 1**, (3 dc, ch 2, 3 dc) in next pc *(corner)*, rep from * around, ending last rep at **, join in 3rd ch of beg ch-3. Fasten off.

Rnd 5: Join next color in any corner ch sp, ch 3, (2 dc, ch 2, 3 dc) in same ch sp, *[ch 1, 3 dc in next ch sp] 3 times, ch 1**, (3 dc, ch 2, 3 dc) in next ch sp, rep from * around, ending last rep at **, join in 3rd ch of beg ch-3. Fasten off.

Rnd 6: Join first color with sc in any corner ch sp, 2 sc in same ch sp, sc in each st and in each ch-1 sp around with 3 sc in each corner ch sp, join in beg sc. Fasten off. ■

Square 48

FINISHED SIZE
5 inches square

GAUGE
Rnds 1 & 2 = 2½ inches in diameter

PATTERN NOTES
Chain-3 at beginning of row or round counts as first double crochet unless otherwise stated.

Join with slip stitch as indicated unless otherwise stated.

Square is made with 2 colors of medium (worsted) weight yarn.

INSTRUCTIONS
SQUARE
Rnd 1: With size H hook, ch 6, sl st in first ch to form ring, **ch 3** *(see Pattern Notes)*, 15 dc in ring, **join** *(see Pattern Notes)* in 3rd ch of beg ch-3. Fasten off.

Rnd 2: Join next color with **bp sl st** *(see Stitch Guide)* around any st, ch 3, **bpdc** *(see Stitch Guide)* around same st, ch 3, sk next st, [2 bpdc around next st, ch 3, sk next st] around, join in 3rd ch of beg ch-3. Fasten off.

Rnd 3: Join first color in any ch sp, ch 3, (dc, ch 3, 2 dc) in same ch sp, *(corner)*, *3 dc in next ch sp**, (2 dc, ch 3, 2 dc) in next ch sp *(corner)*, join in 3rd ch of beg ch-3. Fasten off.

Rnd 4: Join 2nd color in any corner ch sp, ch 2 *(counts as first hdc)*, (hdc, ch 2, 2 hdc) in same corner ch sp, hdc in each st around with (2 hdc, ch 2, 2 hdc) in each corner ch sp, join in 2nd ch of beg ch-2. Fasten off.

Rnd 5: Join first color in any corner ch sp, ch 3, (dc, ch 2, 2 dc) in same corner ch sp, dc in each st around with (2 dc, ch 2, 2 dc) in each corner ch sp, join in 3rd ch of beg ch-3. Fasten off. ■

Square 49

FINISHED SIZE
8 inches square

GAUGE
Rnd 1 = 2 inches in diameter

PATTERN NOTES
Chain-3 at beginning of row or round counts as first double crochet unless otherwise stated.

Join with slip stitch as indicated unless otherwise stated.

Square is made with 1 color of medium (worsted) weight yarn.

INSTRUCTIONS
SQUARE
Rnd 1: With size H hook, ch 8, sl st in first ch to form ring, ch 4 *(counts as first tr)*, 15 tr in ring, join in 4th ch of beg ch-4.

Rnd 2: Ch 1, sk first st, (sc, hdc, dc, tr, dc, hdc, sc) in next st, [sk next st, (sc, hdc, dc, tr, dc, hdc, sc) in next st] around, join in beg sc.

Rnd 3: Ch 1, sl st in each of next 2 sts, (**bpsc, bphdc, bpdc, 2 bptr,** bpdc, bphdc, bpsc)

around each tr around *(see Stitch Guide for all bp sts)*, join in beg bpsc.

Rnd 4: Sl st in each of first 3 sts, sc in sp between this tr and next tr, **ch 3** *(see Pattern Notes)*, (2 dc, ch 3, 3 dc) in same place, *ch 2, (3 dc, {ch 2, 3 dc} twice) in sp between 2 bptr of next group, ch 2*, (3 dc, ch 3, 3 dc) in next sp between 2 bptr of next group, rep from * around, ending last rep at **, join in 3rd ch of beg ch-3.

Rnd 5: Sl st in each of next 2 sts, sl st in next ch sp, ch 3, 2 dc in same ch sp, 3 dc in each of next 2 ch sps, *(3 dc, ch 3, 3 dc) (corner) in next ch sp**, 3 dc in each of next 5 ch sps, rep from * around, ending last rep at **, 3 dc in each of last 2 ch sp, join in 3rd ch of beg ch-3.

Rnd 6: Ch 3, dc in each st around with (3 dc, ch 3, 3 dc) (corner) in each ch sp, join in 3rd ch of beg ch-3. Fasten off. ∎

Square 50

FINISHED SIZE
8 inches square

GAUGE
Rnds 1 & 2 = 3¼ inches

PATTERN NOTES

Join with slip stitch as indicated unless otherwise stated.

Chain-3 at beginning of row or round counts as first double crochet unless otherwise stated.

Square is made with 1 color of medium (worsted) weight yarn.

SPECIAL STITCHES

Beginning cluster (beg cl): Ch 3 *(counts as first dc)*, holding back last lp of each st on hook, 2 dc in place indicated, yo, pull through all lps on hook.

Cluster (cl): Holding back last lp of each st on hook, 3 dc in place indicated, yo, pull through all lps on hook.

INSTRUCTIONS
SQUARE

Rnd 1: With size H hook, ch 6, sl st in first ch to form ring, **beg cl** *(see Special Stitches)* in ring, ch 3, [**cl** *(see Special Stitches)* in ring, ch 3] 7 times, **join** *(see Pattern Notes)* in beg cl. *(8 cls, 8 ch sps)*

Rnd 2: Sl st in first ch sp, ch 4 *(counts as first dc and ch-1)*, *(cl ch 3, cl) in next ch sp *(corner)*, ch 1**, dc in next ch sp, ch 1, rep from * around, ending last rep at **, join in 3rd ch of beg ch-4.

Rnd 3: **Ch 3** *(see Pattern Notes)*, *dc in next ch sp, ch 1, (cl, ch 3, cl) in next corner ch sp, ch 1, dc in next ch sp**, dc in next st, rep from * around, ending last rep at **, join in 3rd ch of beg ch-3.

Rnd 4: Ch 3, dc in next st, *dc in next ch sp, ch 1, (cl, ch 3, cl) in next corner ch sp, ch 1, dc in next ch sp**, dc in each of next 3 sts, rep from * around, ending last rep at **, dc in last st, join in 3rd ch of beg ch-3.

Rnd 5: Ch 1, **fpsc** *(see Stitch Guide)* around first st, ch 5, [fpsc around next st, ch 5] around, join in beg fpsc. Fasten off.

Rnd 6: Working in sts on rnd 4, join in any corner ch sp, ch 3, 2 dc in same ch sp, *dc in each st and ch-1 sp across to next corner ch sp**, (3 dc, ch 2, 3 dc) in next corner ch sp, rep from * around, ending last rep at **, 3 dc in first ch sp worked in, ch 1, join with sc in 3rd ch of beg ch-3 forming last ch sp.

Rnd 7: Ch 3, 2 dc in this ch sp, *sk next st, dc in each of next 13 sts, sk next st**, (3 dc, ch 2, 3 dc) in next corner ch sp, rep from *around, ending last rep at **, 3 dc in first ch sp worked in, ch 2, join in 3rd ch of beg ch-3.

Rnd 8: Ch 1, fpsc around first st, ch 5, [fpsc around next st, ch 5] around, join in beg fpsc. Fasten off.

Rnd 9: Working in sts on rnd 7, join in any corner ch sp, ch 3, (2 dc in same ch sp, ch 2, 3 dc) in same ch sp, *sk next 2 sts, dc in each of next 15 sts, sk next 2 sts**, (3 dc, ch 2, 3 dc) in next corner ch sp, rep from * around, ending last rep at **, join in 3rd ch of beg ch-3. Fasten off. ■

Square 51

FINISHED SIZE
6½ inches square

GAUGE
Rnds 1 & 2 = 2¾ inches

PATTERN NOTES
Join with slip stitch as indicated unless otherwise stated.

Square is made with 1 color of medium (worsted) weight yarn.

SPECIAL STITCHES
Beginning cluster (beg cl): Ch 3 *(counts as first dc)*, holding back last lp of each st on hook, 2 dc in place indicated, yo, pull through all lps on hook.

Cluster (cl): Holding back last lp of each st on hook, 3 dc in place indicated, yo, pull through all lps on hook.

INSTRUCTIONS
SQUARE
Rnd 1: With size H hook, ch 5, sl st in first ch to form ring, ch 1, 16 sc in ring, **join** *(see Pattern Notes)* in beg sc.

Rnd 2: **Beg cl** *(see Special Stitches)* in first st, ch 3, sk next st, [**cl** *(see Special Stitches)* in next st, ch 3, sk next st] around, join in beg cl.

Rnd 3: Beg cl in first cl, *ch 3, sc in next ch sp, ch 3**, cl in next cl, rep from * around, ending last rep at **, join in beg cl.

Rnd 4: Ch 7 *(counts as dc and ch-4)*, dc in same st *(corner)*, *ch 3, dc in next sc, ch 5, sk next cl, dc in next sc, ch 3**, (dc, ch 4, dc) in next cl *(corner)*, rep from * around, ending last rep at **, join in 3rd ch of beg ch-7.

Rnd 5: (Beg cl, ch 3, cl) in first st, *ch 3, (cl, ch 3, cl) in next st, ch 3, cl in next st, ch 3, cl in next ch sp, ch 3, cl in next st, ch 3**, (cl, ch 3, cl) in next st, rep from * around, ending last rep at **, join in beg cl.

Rnd 6: Ch 1, sc in first st, *ch 4, sk next ch sp and next cl, (cl, ch 3, cl) in next ch sp, ch 4, sk next cl and next ch sp, [sc in next cl, ch 4] 4 times**, sc in next cl, rep from * around, ending last rep at **, join in beg sc. Fasten off. ∎

Square 52

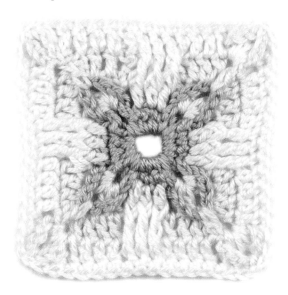

FINISHED SIZE
5 inches square

GAUGE
Rnd 1 = 1½ inches in diameter

PATTERN NOTES
Chain-3 at beginning of row or round counts as first double crochet unless otherwise stated.

Join with slip stitch as indicated unless otherwise stated.

Square is made with 3 colors of medium (worsted) weight yarn.

INSTRUCTIONS
SQUARE
Rnd 1: With size H hook, ch 6, sl st in first ch to form ring, ch 1, [4 sc in ring *(place marker)*, ch 5, sl st in ring] 4 times, **join** *(see Pattern Notes)* in beg sc.

Rnd 2: Ch 1, sc in each of first 3 sts, sk next st, *working behind ch-5, (sl st, ch 12, sl st) in ring at marker, sk next st**, sc in each of next 3 sts, rep from * around, ending last rep at **, join in beg sc. Fasten off.

Rnd 3: Push each ch-5 to the back through ch-12, join next color with sl st in any ch-5 sp, **ch 3** *(see Pattern Notes)*, (dc, ch 2, 2 dc) in same ch sp, *dc in each of next 3 sc**, (2 dc, ch 2, 2 dc) in next ch-5 sp, rep from * around, ending last rep at **, join in 3rd ch of beg ch-3.

Rnd 4: Ch 3, dc in next st, *2 dc in next ch sp, dc in next ch-12 sp, ch 8, sl st in top of last dc made, 2 dc in same ch sp on this rnd, dc in each of next 2 sts, ch 3, sk next 3 sts**, dc in each of next 2 sts, rep from * around, ending last rep at **, join in 3rd ch of beg ch-3, Fasten off.

Rnd 5: Join next color in beg st, ch 3, dc in each of next 3 sts, *sk next st, holding ch-8 to front of work, (2 dc, ch 1, 2 dc) in side of sl st at base of ch-8, dc in each of next 4 sts, working in front of next ch-3 sp, **fptr** *(see Stitch Guide)* around each of next 3 sk sts on rnd 3**, dc in each of next 4 sts, rep from * around, ending last rep at **, join in 3rd ch of beg ch-3.

Rnd 6: Ch 1, sc in each st around with sc in both ch-8 sp and ch-1 sp at same time, join in beg sc. Fasten off. ■

Square 53

FINISHED SIZE
5 inches square

GAUGE
Rnds 1 & 2 = 3½ inches

PATTERN NOTES
Join with slip stitch as indicated unless otherwise stated.

Square is made with 1 color and medium (worsted) weight yarn.

SPECIAL STITCH
Puff stitch (puff st): [Yo, insert hook in place indicated, yo pull lp through] 3 times, yo, pull through all lps on hook.

INSTRUCTIONS
SQUARE

Rnd 1: With size H hook, ch 5, sl st in first ch to form ring, ch 5 *(counts as first tr and ch-1)*, [tr in ring, ch 1] 11 times, **join** *(see Pattern Notes)* in 4th ch of beg ch-5. Fasten off.

Rnd 2: Join with sl st in any ch sp, **puff st** *(see Special Stitch)* in same ch sp, ch 1, puff st in same ch sp, ch 1, (puff st, ch 1) twice in each ch sp around, join in beg puff st.

Rnd 3: Sl st in first ch sp, ch 6 *(counts as first tr and ch-2)*, tr in same ch sp, *ch 1, dc in next ch sp, [ch 1, hdc in next ch sp] 3 times, ch 1, dc in next ch sp, ch 1**, (tr, ch 2, tr) in next ch sp, rep from * around, ending last rep at **, join in 4th ch of beg ch-6.

Rnd 4: Sl st in first ch sp, ch 1, (3 sc, ch 2, 3 sc) in same ch sp, *2 sc in each of next 6 ch sps**, (3 sc, ch 3, 3 sc) in next ch sp, rep from * around, ending last rep at **, join in beg sc. Fasten off. ■

Square 54

FINISHED SIZE
6½ inches square

GAUGE
Rnd 1 = 1½ inches in diameter

PATTERN NOTES
Chain-3 at beginning of row or round counts as first double crochet unless otherwise stated.

Join with slip stitch as indicated unless otherwise stated.

Square is made with 3 colors of medium (worsted) weight yarn.

Always change colors in last stitch made.

INSTRUCTIONS
SQUARE
Rnd 1: With size H hook, ch 5, sl st in first ch to form ring, **ch 3** *(see Pattern Notes)*, 5 dc in ring **changing colors** *(see Pattern Notes and Stitch Guide)* in last st, 6 dc in ring, **join** *(see Pattern Notes)* in 3rd ch of beg ch-3.

Rnd 2: Ch 3, (dc, ch 2, 2 dc) in same st *(corner)*, dc in each of next 2 sts, (2 dc, ch 2, 2 dc) in next st *(corner)*, dc in each of next 2 sts, changing to first color, [(2 dc, ch 2, 2 dc) in next st *(corner)*, dc in each of next 2 sts] twice, join in 3rd ch of beg ch-3.

Rnd 3: Ch 3, dc in next st, (2 dc, ch 2, 2 dc) in next ch sp, dc in each of next 6 sts, (2 dc, ch 2, 2 dc) in next ch sp, dc in each of next 4 sts, changing to 2nd color, dc in each of next 2 sts, (2 dc, ch 2, 2 dc) in next ch sp, dc in each of next 6 sts, (2 dc, ch 2, 2 dc) in next ch sp, dc in each of last 4 sts, join in 3rd ch of beg ch-3.

Rnd 4: Ch 3, dc in each of next 3 sts, (2 dc, ch 2, 2 dc) in next corner ch sp, dc in each of next 10 sts, (2 dc, ch 2, 2 dc) in next ch sp, dc in each of next 6 sts, changing to first color in last st, dc in each of next 4 sts, (2 dc, ch 2, 2 dc) in next ch sp, dc in each of next 10 sts, (2 dc, ch 2, 2 dc) in next ch sp, dc in each of last 6 sts, join in 3rd ch of beg ch-3.

Rnd 5: Ch 3, dc in each of next 5 sts, (2 dc, ch 2, 2 dc) in next corner ch sp, dc in each of next 14 sts, (2 dc, ch 2, 2 dc) in next ch sp, dc in each of next 8 sts, changing to 2nd color in last st, dc in each of next 6 sts, (2 dc, ch 2, 2 dc) in next ch sp, dc in each of next 14 sts, (2 dc, ch 2, 2 dc) in next ch sp, dc in each of last 8 sts, join in 3rd ch of beg ch-3. Fasten off.

Rnd 6: Join 3rd color with sc in any corner ch sp, 2 sc in same ch sp, sc in each st around with 3 sc in each corner ch sp, join in beg sc. Fasten off. ∎

Square 55

FINISHED SIZE
5 inches square

GAUGE
Rnd 1 = 2 inches in diameter

PATTERN NOTES
Chain-3 at beginning of row or round counts as first double crochet unless otherwise stated.

Join with slip stitch as indicated unless otherwise stated.

Square is made with 4 colors of medium (worsted) weight yarn.

INSTRUCTIONS
SQUARE
Rnd 1: With size H hook, ch 8, sl st in first ch to form ring, **ch 3** (see Pattern Notes), 3 dc in ring, [ch 3, 4 dc in ring] 3 times, ch 3, **join** (see Pattern Notes) in 3rd ch of beg ch-3. Fasten off.

Rnd 2: Join next color in any ch-3 sp, ch 3, 4 dc in same ch sp (corner), *fpdc dec (see Stitch Guide) around next 2 sts, sk next st behind fpdc dec, dc in **back lp** (see Stitch Guide) of last st worked around, dc in back lp of next st, fpdc dec around last st worked in and next st**,

5 dc in next ch sp (corner), rep from * around, ending last rep at **, join in 3rd ch of beg ch-3. Fasten off.

Rnd 3: Join next color with sc in center corner dc, 2 sc in same st, *working over st on last rnd, 2 dc in ch sp on rnd 1, sk 2 sts behind last 2 sts on this rnd, sc in each of next 4 sts, working over st on last rnd, 2 dc in ch sp on rnd 1, sk 2 sts behind last 2 sts on this rnd**, 3 sc in next st, rep from * around, ending last rep at **, join in beg sc. Fasten off.

Rnd 4: Join next color with sc in center corner st, 2 sc in same st, *sc in each of next 2 sts, fpdc around both of next 2 dc at same time, sc in each of next 6 sts, fpdc around both of next 2 dc at same time, sc in each of next 2 sts**, 3 sc in center corner st, rep from * around, ending last rep at **, join in beg sc. Fasten off.

Rnd 5: Join first color with sc in center corner st, 2 sc in same st, sc in each st around with 3 sc in each center corner st, join in beg sc. Fasten off. ■

Square 56

FINISHED SIZE
8 inches point to point

GAUGE
Rnd 1 = 1 inch in diameter

PATTERN NOTES
Chain-3 at beginning of row or round counts as first double crochet unless otherwise stated.

Join with slip stitch as indicated unless otherwise stated.

Square is made with 4 colors of medium (worsted) weight yarn.

SPECIAL STITCHES
Beginning cluster (beg cl): Ch 3 (*counts as first dc*), holding back last lp of each st on hook, 3 dc in place indicated, yo, pull through all lps on hook.

Cluster (cl): Holding back last lp of each st on hook, 4 dc in place indicated, yo, pull through all lps on hook.

INSTRUCTIONS
SQUARE
Rnd 1: With size H hook, ch 2, 8 sc in 2nd ch from hook, **join** (*see Pattern Notes*) in beg sc. Fasten off.

Rnd 2: Join next color in any st, **beg cl** (*see Special Stitches*) in same st, ch 3, [**cl** (*see Special Stitches*) in next st, ch 3] around, join in beg cl. Fasten off.

Rnd 3: Join next color with sc in any ch sp, *ch 3, (3 dc, ch 3, 3 dc) in next ch sp (*corner*), ch 3**, sc in next ch sp, rep from * around, ending last rep at **, join in beg sc. Fasten off.

Rnd 4: Join next color in any corner ch sp, **ch 3** (*see Pattern Notes*), (dc, ch 2, 2 dc) in same ch sp, *dc in each of next 2 sts, ch 3, sk next st, [sc in next ch sp, ch 3] twice, sk next st, dc in each of next 2 sts**, (2 dc, ch 2, 2 dc) in next corner ch sp, rep from * around, ending last rep at **, join in 3rd ch of beg ch-3.

Rnd 5: Ch 3, dc in next st, *(2 dc, ch 3, 2 dc) in next corner ch sp, *dc in each of next 2 sts, ch 3, sk next 2 sts, [sc in next ch sp, ch 3] 3 times,

sk next 2 sts**, dc in each of next 2 sts, rep from * around, ending last rep at **, join in 3rd ch of beg ch-3. Fasten off. ∎

Square 57

FINISHED SIZE
6 inches square

GAUGE
Rnds 1 & 2 = 2¼ inches in diameter

PATTERN NOTES
Chain-3 at beginning of row or round counts as first double crochet unless otherwise stated.

Join with slip stitch as indicated unless otherwise stated.

Square is made with 4 colors of medium (worsted) weight yarn.

SPECIAL STITCHES
Beginning cluster (beg cl): Ch 3 (*counts as first dc*), holding back last lp of each st on hook, 3 dc in place indicated, yo, pull through all lps on hook.

Cluster (cl): Holding back last lp of each st on hook, 4 dc in place indicated, yo, pull through all lps on hook.

INSTRUCTIONS
SQUARE

Rnd 1: With size H hook, ch 4, sl st in first ch to form ring, ch 1, 8 sc in ring, **join** (see Pattern Notes) in beg sc. Fasten off.

Rnd 2: Join next color in any st, **beg cl** (see Special Stitches) in same st, ch 2, [**cl** (see Special Stitches) in next st, ch 2] around, join in beg cl. Fasten off.

Rnd 3: Join next color in any ch sp, ch 5 (counts as first dc and ch-2), (dc, ch 2, dc) in same ch sp, ch 2, (dc, ch 2, dc) in next ch sp, *ch 2, (dc, {ch 2, dc} twice) in next ch sp (corner), ch 2, (dc, ch 2, dc) in next ch sp, rep from * around, ch 2, join in 3rd ch of beg ch-5. Fasten off.

Rnd 4: Join next color with sc in any ch sp, sc in same ch sp, 2 sc in each ch sp around, with ch 3 at each corner, join in beg sc.

Rnd 5: **Ch 3** (see Pattern Notes), dc in each st around with (2 dc, ch 3, 2 dc) in each corner ch sp, join in 3rd ch of beg ch-3.

Rnd 6: Ch 3, dc in each st around with (2 dc, ch 3, 2 dc) in each corner ch sp, join in 3rd ch of beg ch-3. Fasten off. ■

Square 58

FINISHED SIZE
4½ inches square

GAUGE
Rnds 1 & 2 = 2¾ inches

PATTERN NOTES
Join with slip stitch as indicated unless otherwise stated.

Square is made with 4 colors of medium (worsted) weight yarn.

SPECIAL STITCHES
Puff stitch (puff st): [Yo, insert hook in place indicated, yo pull lp through] 3 times, yo, pull through all lps on hook.

Beginning popcorn (beg pc): Ch 3 (counts as first dc), 4 dc in place indicated, drop lp from hook, insert hook in 3rd ch of beg ch-3, pull dropped lp through, ch 1 to secure.

Popcorn (pc): 5 dc in place indicated, drop lp from hook, insert hook in first dc of group, pull dropped lp through, ch 1 to secure.

INSTRUCTIONS
SQUARE

Rnd 1: With size H hook, ch 5, sl st in first ch to form ring, ch 1, sc in ring, ch 1, [sc in ring, ch 1] 11 times, **join** (see Pattern Notes) in beg sc. Fasten off.

Rnd 2: Join next color in any ch sp, ch 1, **puff st** (see Special Stitches) in same ch sp, ch 3, [puff st in next ch sp, ch 3] around, join in beg puff st. Fasten off.

Rnd 3: Join next color in any ch sp, (**beg pc**—see Special Stitches, ch 3, **pc**—see Special Stitches in same ch sp (corner), *[ch 3, dc in next ch sp] twice, ch 3**, (pc, ch 3, pc) in next ch sp, rep from * around, ending last rep at **, join in 3rd ch of beg ch-3. Fasten off.

Rnd 4: Join next color in any corner ch sp, ch 3 (counts as first dc), (2 dc, ch 1, 3 dc) in same ch sp, *3 dc in each of next 3 ch sps**, (3 dc, ch 1, 3 dc) in next ch sp, rep from * around, ending last rep at **, join in 3rd ch of beg ch-3. Fasten off. ■

Square 59

FINISHED SIZE
5½ inches square

GAUGE
Rnds 1 & 2 = 2½ inches

PATTERN NOTES
Chain-3 at beginning of row or round counts as first double crochet unless otherwise stated.

Join with slip stitch as indicated unless otherwise stated.

Square is made with 2 colors of medium (worsted) weight yarn.

INSTRUCTIONS
SQUARE
Rnd 1: With size H hook, ch 6, sl st in first ch to form ring, **ch 3** (*see Pattern Notes*), 11 dc in ring, **join** (*see Pattern Notes*) in 3rd ch of beg ch-3. Fasten off.

Rnd 2: Join next color in sp between any sts, ch 3, 3 dc in same sp, *sk next st, **fptr** (*see Stitch Guide*) around next st, sk next st**, 4 dc in next sp between sts, rep from * around, ending last rep at **, join in 3rd ch of beg ch-3.

Rnd 3: Ch 3, *2 dc in next st, ch 1 (*corner*), 2 dc in next st, dc in next st, 3 fptr around next fptr**, dc in next st, rep from * around, ending last rep at **, join in 3rd ch of beg ch-3.

Rnd 4: Sl st in each of next 2 sts, sl st in next corner ch sp, ch 3, (3 dc, ch 1, 4 dc) in same ch sp, *sk next 4 sts, 4 dc in center fptr, sk next 4 sts**, (4 dc, ch 1, 4 dc) in next corner ch sp, rep from * around, ending last rep at **, join in 3rd ch of beg ch-3. Fasten off.

Rnd 5: Join first color in any corner ch sp, ch 3, (3 dc, ch 1, 4 dc) in same ch sp, *3 dc in sp between next dc groups, fptr around center fptr on rnd 3, 3 dc in sp between next dc groups**, (4 dc, ch 1, 4 dc) in next corner ch sp, rep from * around, ending last rep at **, join in 3rd ch of beg ch-3. Fasten off.

Rnd 6: Join 2nd color with sc in any corner ch sp, 2 sc in same ch sp, sc in each st around with 3 sc in each corner ch sp, join in beg sc. Fasten off. ■

Square 60

FINISHED SIZE
7 inches square

GAUGE
Rnds 1 & 2 = 2½ inches

PATTERN NOTES
Join with slip stitch as indicated unless otherwise stated.

Chain-3 at beginning of row or round counts as first double crochet unless otherwise stated.

Square is made with 3 colors of medium (worsted) weight yarn.

SPECIAL STITCHES
Beginning popcorn (beg pc): Ch 3 *(counts as first dc)*, 4 dc in place indicated, drop lp from hook, insert hook in 3rd ch of beg ch-3, pull dropped lp through, ch 1 to secure.

Popcorn (pc): 5 dc in place indicated, drop lp from hook, insert hook in first dc of group, pull dropped lp through, ch 1 to secure.

INSTRUCTIONS
SQUARE
Rnd 1: With size H hook, ch 4, sl st in first ch to form ring, **beg pc** *(see Special Stitches)* in ring,

ch 3, [**pc** *(see Special Stitches)* in ring, ch 3] 3 times, **join** *(see Special Stitches)* in beg pc.

Rnd 2: Sl st in first ch sp, (beg pc, ch 3, pc) in same ch sp, ch 3, [(pc, ch 3, pc) in next ch sp, ch 3] around, join in beg pc.

Rnd 3: Sl st in first ch sp, (beg pc, ch 3, pc) in same ch sp, ch 3, [(pc, ch 3, pc) in next ch sp, ch 3] around, join in beg pc. Fasten off.

Rnd 4: Join next color in any ch sp, ch 4 *(counts as first tr)*, (2 tr, ch 2, 3 tr) in same ch sp *(corner)*, *3 dc in each of next 3 ch sps**, (3 tr, ch 3, 3 tr) in next ch sp *(corner)*, rep from * around, ending last rep at **, join in 4th ch of beg ch-4. Fasten off.

Rnd 5: Join next color in any corner ch sp, ch 4 *(counts as first dc and ch-1)*, (dc, {ch 1, dc} twice) in same ch sp, *sk next st, [(dc, ch 1, dc) in next st, sk next 2 sts] 4 times, (dc, ch 1, dc) in next st, sk next st**, (dc, {ch 1, dc} 3 times) in next ch sp, rep from * around, ending last rep at **, join in 3rd ch of beg ch-4.

Rnd 6: Sl st in first ch sp, ch 4, dc in same ch sp, *(dc, {ch 1, dc} 3 times) in next ch sp**, (dc, ch 1, dc) in each of next 7 ch sps, rep from * around, ending last rep at **, (dc, ch 1, dc) in each ch sp around, join in 3rd ch of beg ch-4. Fasten off. ∎

Square 61

FINISHED SIZE
6 inches square

GAUGE
Rnd 1 = 1¾ inches in diameter

PATTERN NOTES
Chain-3 at beginning of row or round counts as first double crochet unless otherwise stated.

Join with slip stitch as indicated unless otherwise stated.

Square is made with 3 colors of medium (worsted) weight yarn.

INSTRUCTIONS
SQUARE
Rnd 1: With size H hook, ch 4, sl st in first ch to form ring, **ch 3** (see Pattern Notes), 15 dc in ring, **join** (see Pattern Notes) in 3rd ch of beg ch-3.

Rnd 2: Ch 1, sc in first st, ch 5, sk next st, [sc in next st, ch 5, sk next st] around, join in beg sc. Fasten off.

Rnd 3: Working behind ch-5 sps in sk sts on rnd 1, join next color in any sk st on rnd 1, ch 4 (counts as first dc and ch-1), dc in same st, ch 1, [(dc, ch 1, dc) in next sk st on rnd 1, ch 1] around, join in 3rd ch of beg ch-4. Fasten off.

Rnd 4: Working in ch-5 sps of rnd 2 and ch-1 sps of rnd 3 at same time, join next color in any ch sp, ch 4 (counts as first tr), 2 tr in same ch sp (corner), *3 dc in next ch-1 sp on rnd 3, dc in ch-5 sp and ch-1 sp at same time, 3 dc in next ch-1 sp on rnd 3**, 3 tr in next ch-5 sp and ch-1 sp at same time, rep from * around, ending last rep at **, join in 4th ch of beg ch-4. Fasten off.

Rnd 5: Join first color with sc in center tr of any corner, ch 5, sc in same st, *[ch 5, sk next st, sc in next st] 4 times, ch 5, sk next st**, (sc, ch 5, sc) in center corner st, rep from * around, ending last rep at **, join in beg sc. Fasten off.

Rnd 6: Holding ch-5 sps to front and working in sk sts on rnd 4, join 2nd color in last sk st on rnd 4, ch 3, dc in same st, ch 5 (corner), *2 dc in each of next 5 sk sts**, ch 5 (corner), rep from * around, ending last rep at **, 2 dc in each sk st around, join in 3rd ch of beg ch-3. Fasten off.

Rnd 7: Working in corner ch-5 sps on rnds 5 and 6 at same time, join 3rd color in any corner ch sp, ch 3, 4 dc in same ch sp, *working in 2nd dc of group and ch-5 sps on rnd 5 at same time, 2 dc in each 2nd dc of group and ch-5 sp at same time across to next corner ch sps**, 5 dc in ch-5 sps of rnds 5 and 6 at same time, rep from * around, ending last rep at **, join in 3rd ch of beg ch-3. Fasten off. ■

Square 62

FINISHED SIZE
4¾ inches square

GAUGE
Rnds 1 & 2 = 2 inches

PATTERN NOTES
Join with slip stitch as indicated unless otherwise stated.

Square is made with 4 colors of medium (worsted) weight yarn.

INSTRUCTIONS
SQUARE

Rnd 1: With size H hook, ch 4, sl st in first ch to form ring, ch 1, [sc in ring, ch 5] 5 times, **join** *(see Pattern Notes)* in beg sc. Fasten off.

Rnd 2: Working behind ch-5 sps, join next color with sc in ring between any 2 sts, sc in same sp, ch 1, [2 sc in ring between next 2 sts, ch 1] around, join in beg sc. Fasten off.

Rnd 3: Join next color with sc in any ch sp, ch 3, sk next 2 sts, [sc in next ch sp, ch 3, sk next 2 sts] around, join in beg sc.

Rnd 4: Sl st in first ch sp, ch 1, (sc, ch 3) twice in same ch sp and in each ch sp around, join in beg sc.

Rnd 5: Sl st in first ch sp, ch 1, sc in same ch sp, *(2 dc, ch 3, 2 dc) in next ch sp *(corner)**, sc in next ch sp, rep from * around, ending last rep at **, join in beg sc.

Rnd 6: Sl st in each st across to and in next ch sp, ch 1, (sc, ch 5, sc) in same ch sp *(corner)*, *[ch 1, sk next st, sc in next st] twice, ch 1, sk next st**, (sc, ch 5, sc) in next ch sp *(corner)*, rep from * around, ending last rep at **, join in beg sc. Fasten off.

Rnd 7: Join next color in any corner ch sp, ch 3 *(counts as first dc)*, (2 dc, ch 3, 3 dc) in same ch sp, [ch 1, 3 dc in next ch sp] 3 times, ch 1**, (3 dc, ch 3, 3 dc) in next corner ch sp, rep from * around, ending last rep at **, join in 3rd ch of beg ch-3. Fasten off.

Rnd 8: Join first color with sc in any corner ch sp, 2 sc in same ch sp, *[ch 3, sc in next ch sp] 4 times, ch 3**, 3 sc in next corner ch sp, rep from * around, ending last rep at **, join in beg sc. Fasten off. ∎

Square 63

FINISHED SIZE
6 inches square

GAUGE
Rnds 1–3 = 2½ inches

PATTERN NOTES
Join with slip stitch as indicated unless otherwise stated.

Chain-3 at beginning of row or round counts as first double crochet unless otherwise stated.

Square is made with 3 colors of medium (worsted) weight yarn.

INSTRUCTIONS
SQUARE

Rnd 1: With size H hook, ch 2, 8 sc in 2nd ch from hook, **join** *(see Pattern Notes)* in beg sc.

Rnd 2: Ch 1, sc in first st, *ch 6, 3 sc in 2nd ch from hook and in each of next 4 chs *(petal)**, sc in next st, rep from * around, ending last rep at **, join in beg sc.

Rnd 3: Ch 1, sc in first sc, *ch 3, sk next petal**, sc in next sc, rep from * around, ending last rep at **, join in beg sc. Fasten off.

Rnd 4: Join next color with sc in any ch sp, *ch 7, sl st in 2nd ch from hook, sc in each of next 2 chs, 2 hdc in next ch, hdc in each of last 2 chs, sl st in same ch sp *(leaf)* **, [ch 1, sc in next ch sp] twice, rep from * around, ending last rep at **, ch 1, sc in last ch sp, ch 1, join in beg sc. Fasten off.

Rnd 5: Join next color with sc in any ch-1 sp after leaf, **ch 3** *(see Pattern Notes)*, *working over next st, 3 dc in next ch sp on rnd 3, dc in next ch-1 sp on this rnd, working behind leaf, (2 dc, ch 3, 2 dc) in next ch sp on rnd 3**, dc in next ch-1 sp on this rnd, rep from * around, ending last rep at **, join in 3rd ch of beg ch-3.

Rnd 6: Ch 3, dc in each st around with 5 dc in each corner ch sp, join in 3rd ch of beg ch-3.

Rnd 7: Ch 3 *(counts as first hdc and ch-1)*, [sk next st, hdc in next st, ch 1] 4 times, *(hdc, ch 1, hdc) in next st**, [ch 1, sk next st, hdc in next st] 6 times, ch 1, sk next st, rep from * around, ending last rep at **, ch 1, sk next st, [hdc in next st, ch 1, sk next st] around, join in 2nd ch of beg ch-3. Fasten off.

Rnd 8: Join 2nd color with sc in any corner ch sp, sc in same ch sp, *ch 1, [sc in next ch sp, ch 1] 7 times**, 2 sc in next corner ch sp, rep from * around, ending last rep at **, join in beg sc. Fasten off. ■

Square 64

FINISHED SIZE
6 inches square

GAUGE
Rnd 1 = 3 inches in diameter

PATTERN NOTES
Join with slip stitch as indicated unless otherwise stated.

Chain-3 at beginning of row or round counts as first double crochet unless otherwise stated.

Square is made with 4 colors of worsted (weight) yarn.

SPECIAL STITCH
Popcorn (pc): 5 tr in place indicated, drop lp from hook, insert hook in first dc of group, pull dropped lp through, ch 1 to secure.

INSTRUCTIONS
SQUARE
Rnd 1: With size H hook, ch 4, sl st in first ch to form ring, [ch 4, 3 tr in ring, ch 4, sl st in ring *(petal)*] 4 times. Fasten off.

Rnd 2: Join next color with sc in center tr of any tr group, *ch 3, working between petals, tr in ring on rnd 1, ch 3**, sc in center tr of next tr group, rep from * around, ending last rep at **, **join** *(see Pattern Notes)* in beg sc.

Rnd 3: Ch 1, sc in first st, *ch 3, **pc** *(see Special Stitch)* in next ch sp, ch 3**, sc in next st, rep from * around, ending last rep at **, join in beg sc. Fasten off.

Rnd 4: Join next color in first st, **ch 3** *(see Pattern Notes)*, 3 dc in same st, *sc in next pc, (3 tr, ch 3, 3 tr) in next sc *(corner)*, sc in next pc**, 4 dc in next sc, rep from * around, ending last rep at **, join in 3rd ch of beg ch-3. Fasten off.

Rnd 5: Join next color in any corner ch sp, ch 3, (2 dc, ch 3, 3 dc) in same ch sp, dc in each st around with (3 dc, ch 3, 3 dc) in each corner ch sp, join in 3rd ch of beg ch-3. Fasten off. ■

Square 65

FINISHED SIZE
7½ inches square

GAUGE
Rnds 1–3 = 3 inches in diameter

PATTERN NOTES
Join with slip stitch as indicated unless otherwise stated.

Chain-3 at beginning of row or round counts as first double crochet unless otherwise stated.

Square is made with 3 colors of medium (worsted) weight yarn.

SPECIAL STITCHES
Long single crochet (lng sc): Insert hook in place indicated, pull up long lp, complete sc.

V-stitch (V-st): (Dc, ch 1, dc) in place indicated.

INSTRUCTIONS
SQUARE
Rnd 1: With size H hook, ch 4, sl st in first ch to form ring, ch 1, 12 sc in ring, **join** (see Pattern Notes) in beg sc. Fasten off.

Rnd 2: Join next color with sc in any st, **ch 3** (see Pattern Notes), tr in same st, *(tr, dc) in next st, sc in next st**, (dc, tr) in next st, rep from * around, ending last rep at **, join in 3rd ch of beg ch-3. Fasten off.

Rnd 3: Working over sc in last rnd, join first color with **lng sc** (see Special Stitches) in sc on rnd 1, *[sc in next st, ch 2] 3 times, sc in next st**, working over sc on last rnd, lng sc in next st on rnd 1, rep from * around, ending last rep at **, join in beg sc.

Rnd 4: Ch 6, [sl st in next lng sc, ch 6] around, join in joining sl st of last rnd. Fasten off.

Rnd 5: Join 2nd color with sc in any ch sp, (hdc, 2 dc, 3 tr, 2 dc, hdc, sc) in same ch sp (petal), (sc, hdc, 2 dc, 3 tr, 2 dc, hdc, sc) in each ch sp (petal) around, join in beg sc. Fasten off.

Rnd 6: Join first color with lng sc in any lng sc on rnd 3, [sc in next st, ch 2] 9 times, sc in next st**, lng sc in next st, rep from * around, ending last rep at **, join in beg lng sc. Fasten off.

Rnd 7: Join 2nd color with **fpsc** (see Stitch Guide) around 2nd dc on any petal, *ch 4, sk next 3 tr, fpsc around next dc, ch 4, sl st in back lps of next lng sc, ch 4**, fpsc around 2nd dc of next petal, rep from * around, ending last rep at **, join in beg fpsc. Fasten off.

Rnd 8: Join next color in first ch sp, ch 4 (counts as first dc and ch-1), (dc, 2 **V-sts**—see Special Stitches) in same ch sp, *2 V-sts in each of next 2 ch sps**, 3 V-sts in next ch sp (corner), rep from * around, ending last rep at **, join 3rd ch of beg ch-4.

Rnd 9: Sl st in ch sp of first V-st, ch 4, dc in same ch sp, *(2 dc, ch 3, 2 dc) in ch sp of next V-st (corner)**, V-st in ch sp of each of next 6 V-sts, rep from * around, ending last rep at **, V-st in ch sp of each V-st around, join in 3rd ch of beg ch-4.

Rnd 10: Sl st in ch sp of first V-st, ch 4, dc in same ch sp, *(3 dc, ch 3, 3 dc) in next ch sp (corner)**, V-st in ch sp of each of next 6 V-sts, rep from * around, ending last rep at **, V-st in ch sp of each V-st around, join in 3rd ch of beg ch-4. Fasten off. ∎

Square 66

FINISHED SIZE
5¾ inches square

GAUGE
Rnds 1 & 2 = 1½ inches in diameter

PATTERN NOTES
Join with slip stitch as indicated unless otherwise stated.

Chain-3 at beginning of row or round counts as first double crochet unless otherwise stated.

Square is made with 4 colors of medium (worsted) weight yarn.

SPECIAL STITCH
Long double crochet (lng dc): Yo, insert hook in place indicated, pull up long lp, complete dc.

INSTRUCTIONS
SQUARE
Rnd 1: With size H hook, ch 4, sl st in first ch to form ring, ch 1, 16 sc in ring, **join** (*see Pattern Notes*) in beg sc.

Rnd 2: Ch 1, sc in each of first 2 sts, ch 2, [sc in each of next 2 sts, ch 2] around, join in beg sc.

Rnd 3: Ch 1, sc in each of first 2 sts, ch 3, [sc in each of next 2 sts, ch 3] around, join in beg sc.

Rnd 4: Ch 1, **sc dec** (*see Stitch Guide*) in first 2 sts, ch 3, [sc dec in next 2 sts, ch 3] around, join in beg sc dec. Fasten off.

Rnd 5: Join next color with sc in any st, 2 sc in same st (*corner*), *4 sc in next ch sp, sk next st, 4 sc in next ch sp**, 3 sc in next st (*corner*), rep from * around, ending last rep at **, join in beg sc.

Rnd 6: Ch 1, sc in first st, *3 sc in next st**, sc in each of next 10 sts, rep from * around, ending last rep at **, sc in each st around, join in beg sc.

Rnd 7: Ch 1, sc in each of first 2 sts, *3 sc in next st**, sc in each of next 12 sts, rep from * around, ending last rep at **, sc in each st around, join in beg sc.

Rnd 8: Ch 1, sc in each of first 3 sts, *3 sc in next st**, sc in each of next 14 sts, rep from * around, ending last rep at **, sc in each st around, join in beg sc. Fasten off.

Rnd 9: Join next color with sc in st to left of first st, ch 1, *working over next 5 sts, 5 **lng dc** (*see Special Stitches*) in center sc of rnd 5, ch 1, sk next st on this rnd, [sc in next st, ch 1, sk next st] 5 times**, sc in next st, rep from * around, ending last rep at **, join in beg sc. Fasten off.

Rnd 10: Join 2nd color with sc in center lng dc at any corner, 2 sc in same st, sc in each st and in each ch sp around with 3 sc in each center lng dc corner st, join in beg sc. Fasten off.

Rnd 11: Working in ch sps on rnd 2, join next color in any ch sp, (hdc, 2 dc, hdc) in same ch sp and in each ch sp around, join in beg hdc. Fasten off.

Rnd 12: Working in ch sps on rnd 3, join first color in any ch sp, **ch 3** (*see Pattern Notes*), (2 dc, tr, 3 dc) in same ch sp, (3 dc, tr, 3 dc) in each ch sp around, join in 3rd ch of beg ch-3. Fasten off. ∎

Square 67

FINISHED SIZE
5¼ inches square

GAUGE
Rnd 1 = 1 inch in diameter

PATTERN NOTES
Join with slip stitch as indicated unless otherwise stated.

Chain-3 at beginning of row or round counts as first double crochet unless otherwise stated.

Square is made with 2 colors of medium (worsted) weight yarn.

SPECIAL STITCH
Cluster (cl): Ch 3 *(counts as first dc)*, holding back last lp of each st on hook, 3 dc in 3rd ch from hook, yo, pull through all lps on hook, ch 1 to close.

INSTRUCTIONS
SQUARE
Rnd 1: With size H hook, ch 4, sl st in first ch to form ring, **ch 3** *(see Pattern Notes)*, 2 dc in ring, ch 3, [3 dc in ring, ch 3] 3 times, **join** *(see Pattern Notes)* in 3rd ch of beg ch-3. Fasten off.

Rnd 2: Join next color with sc in any ch sp, ch 3, sc in same ch sp, **cl* *(see Special Stitch)***, (sc, ch 3, sc) in next ch sp, rep from * around, ending last rep at **, join in beg sc. Fasten off.

Rnd 3: Join first color in any ch sp, ch 6 *(counts as first dc and ch-3)*, dc in same ch sp *(corner)*, dc in next st, working behind cl, dc in each of next 3 sts on rnd 2, dc in next st on this rnd**, (dc, ch 3, dc) in next ch sp, rep from * around, ending last rep at **, join in 3rd ch of beg ch-6.

Rnd 4: Join 2nd color with sc in any ch-3 sp, ch 3, sc in same ch sp, **cl, sk next 3 sts, sc in next st, cl, sk next 3 sts**, (sc, ch 3, sc) in next ch sp, rep from * around, ending last rep at **, join in beg sc. Fasten off.

Rnd 5: Join first color in any ch sp, ch 6, dc in same ch sp, **dc in next st, dc in each of next 3 sk sts on rnd 3 behind cl, dc in next st on this rnd, dc in each of next 3 sk sts on rnd 3 behind cl, dc in next st on this rnd**, (dc, ch 3, dc) in next ch sp, rep from * around, ending last rep at **, join in 3rd ch of beg ch-6. Fasten off.

Rnd 6: Join 2nd color with sc in any ch sp, ch 3, sc in same ch sp, **sc in each of next 4 sts, cl, sk next 3 sts, sc in each of next 4 sts**, (sc, ch 3, sc) in next ch sp, rep from * around, ending last rep at **, join in beg sc. Fasten off.

Rnd 7: Join first color with sc in any ch sp, ch 3, sc in same ch sp, **sc in each of next 5 sts, sc in each of next 3 sk sts on rnd 5 behind cl, sc in each of next 5 sts**, (sc, ch 3, sc) in next ch sp, rep from * around, ending last rep at **, join in beg sc. Fasten off. ■

Square 68

FINISHED SIZE
7 inches square

GAUGE
Rnds 1 & 2 = 1½ inches in diameter

PATTERN NOTES
Join with slip stitch as indicated unless otherwise stated.

Chain-3 at beginning of row or round counts as first double crochet unless otherwise stated.

Square is made with 4 colors of medium (worsted) weight yarn.

INSTRUCTIONS
SQUARE
Rnd 1: With size H hook, ch 2, 8 sc in 2nd ch from hook, **join** (see Pattern Notes) in beg sc. Fasten off.

Rnd 2: Join next color with sc in any st, sc in same st, 2 sc in each st around, join in beg sc.

Rnd 3: Ch 1, sc in each of first 3 sts, *ch 3, sk next st**, sc in each of next 3 sts, rep from * around, ending last rep at **, join in beg sc. Fasten off.

Rnd 4: Join next color in any ch sp, *(ch 2, dc, 3 tr, dc, ch 2, sl st) in same ch sp, ch 3, sk next 3 sts**, sl st in next ch sp, rep from * around, ending last rep at **, join in beg sl st. Fasten off.

Rnd 5: Join next color in any ch sp, **ch 3** (see Pattern Notes), 4 dc in same ch sp, *sk next ch-2 sp, sc in each of next 2 sts, 3 sc in next st (corner), sc in each of next 2 sts, sk next ch-2 sp**, 5 dc in next ch sp, rep from * around, ending last rep at **, join in 3rd ch of beg ch-3.

Rnd 6: Ch 1, sc in each of first 8 sts, *3 dc in next st**, sc in each of next 11 sts, rep from * around, ending last rep at **, sc in each st around, join in beg sc. Fasten off.

Rnd 7: Join 3rd color in center corner st, ch 3, 4 dc in same st, *[ch 1, sk next st, hdc in next st] 6 times, ch 1, sk next st**, 5 dc in next st, rep from * around, ending last rep at **, join in 3rd ch of beg ch-3. Fasten off.

Rnd 8: Join first color with sc in center corner st, 2 sc in same st, *sc in each of next 2 sts, [working over ch, sc in sk st on rnd 6, sc in next st on this rnd] 7 times, sc in next st**, 3 sc in next st, rep from * around, ending last rep at **, join in beg sc. Fasten off.

Rnd 9: Join 2nd color in any center corner st, ch 3, 2 dc in same st, dc in each st around, with 3 dc in each center corner st, join in 3rd ch of beg ch-3. Fasten off.

Rnd 10: Join 4th color with sc in any center corner st, 2 sc in same st, sc in each st around with 3 sc in each center corner st, join in beg sc. Fasten off. ■

Square 69

FINISHED SIZE
6½ inches square

GAUGE
3 dc rnds = 1¾ inches

PATTERN NOTES
Join with slip stitch as indicated unless otherwise stated.

Chain-3 at beginning of row or round counts as first double crochet unless otherwise stated.

Square is made with 3 colors of medium (worsted) weight yarn.

SPECIAL STITCHES
Beginning cluster (beg cl): Ch 3 *(counts as first dc)*, holding back last lp of each st on hook, 4 dc in place indicated, yo, pull through all lps on hook.

Cluster (cl): Holding back last lp of each st on hook, 5 dc in place indicated, yo, pull through all lps on hook.

INSTRUCTIONS
SQUARE
Rnd 1: With size H hook, ch 4, sl st in first ch to form ring, ch 1, [sc in ring, ch 3] 8 times, **join** *(see Pattern Notes)* in beg sc.

Rnd 2: Ch 1, sc in first st, ch 5, [sc in next st, ch 5] around, join in beg sc.

Rnd 3: Working in ch sps on rnd 1, sl st in first ch sp, ch 1, (sc, 9 dc, sc) in same ch sp and in each ch sp around, join in beg sc.

Rnd 4: Ch 1, sc in first st, [ch 2, sk next st, sc in next st] 5 times, ch 2**, sc in next st, rep from * around, ending last rep at **, join in beg sc. Fasten off.

Rnd 5: Join next color in any ch sp on rnd 2, **ch 3** *(see Pattern Notes)*, 2 dc in same ch sp,*(3 tr, ch 2, 3 tr) in next ch sp *(corner)**, 3 dc in next ch sp, rep from * around, ending last rep at **, join in 3rd ch of beg ch-3. Fasten off.

Rnd 6: Join next color in any corner ch sp, ch 3, (dc, ch 2, 2 dc) in same ch sp, *dc in each of next 9 sts**, (2 dc, ch 2, 2 dc) in next corner ch sp, rep from * around, ending last rep at **, join in 3rd ch of beg ch-3.

Rnd 7: Ch 5 *(counts as first dc and ch-2)*, sk next st, *5 dc in next ch sp**, [ch 2, sk next st, dc in next st] 6 times, ch 2, sk next st, rep from * around, ending last rep at **, ch 2, sk next st, [dc in next st, ch 2, sk next st] around, join in 3rd ch of beg ch-5. Fasten off.

Rnd 8: Join 2nd color in any corner center st, (**beg cl**—*see Special Stitches*, ch 3, **cl**—*see Special Stitches*) in same st, *sk next st, [dc in next st, dc in next ch sp] 7 times, dc in next st, sk next st**, (cl, ch 3, cl) in next st, rep from * around, ending last rep at **, join in beg cl. Fasten off. ■

Square 70

FINISHED SIZE
5½ inches square

GAUGE
Rnd 1 = 2 inches in diameter

PATTERN NOTES
Join with slip stitch as indicated unless otherwise stated.

Chain-3 at beginning of row or round counts as first double crochet unless otherwise stated.

Square is made with 3 colors of medium (worsted) weight yarn.

SPECIAL STITCHES
Beginning V-stitch (beg V-st): Ch 4 *(counts as first dc and ch-1)*, dc in same st.

V-stitch (V-st): (Dc, ch 1, dc) in place indicated.

INSTRUCTIONS
SQUARE
Rnd 1: With size H hook, ch 4, sl st in first ch to form ring, **ch 3** *(see Pattern Notes)*, 15 dc in ring, **join** *(see Pattern Notes)* in 3rd ch of beg ch-3. Fasten off.

Rnd 2: Join next color with sc in any st, sc in each of next 2 sts, mark last st, ch 5, **turn**, sk last sc worked, sl st in joining sc, turn, 11 sc in ch-5 sp just formed, sl st in marked st, [sc in each of next 2 sts on this rnd, mark last st, ch 5, turn, working behind last lp, sk last 2 sc, sc in next st, 11 sc in ch-5 sp just formed, sl st in marked st] around, working in front of first lp, sl st in 2nd sc of this rnd, mark this st, ch 5, turn, working behind last lp, sk last 2 sc, sc in next st, 11 sc in ch-5 sp just formed, sl st in last marked st. Fasten off.

Rnd 3: Working in **back lps** *(see Stitch Guide)*, join next color in 4th sc of any sc group, **beg V-st** *(see Special Stitches)* in same st, *ch 1, sk next 3 sts, **V-st** *(see Special Stitches)* in next st, ch 1**, V-st in 4th st of next sc group, rep from * around, ending last rep at **, join in 3rd ch of beg ch-3. Fasten off.

Rnd 4: Join first color in any ch sp between V-sts, ch 3, (2 dc, ch 3, 3 dc) in same ch sp *(corner)*, *dc in each of next 7 ch sps**, (3 dc, ch 3, 3 dc) in next ch sp *(corner)*, rep from * around, ending last rep at **, join in 3rd ch of beg ch-3. Fasten off.

Rnd 5: Join 2nd color with sc in any ch sp, 2 sc in same ch sp, sc in each st around with 3 sc in each corner ch sp, join in beg sc. Fasten off. ∎

Square 71

FINISHED SIZE
4 inches square

GAUGE
Rnd 1 = 1 inch in diameter

PATTERN NOTES
Join with slip stitch as indicated unless otherwise stated.

Chain-3 at beginning of row or round counts as first double crochet unless otherwise stated.

Square is made with 4 colors of medium (worsted) weight yarn.

INSTRUCTIONS
SQUARE
Rnd 1: With size H hook, ch 4, sl st in first ch to form ring, ch 1, [sc in ring, ch 2] 4 times, **join** (*see Pattern Notes*) in beg sc. Fasten off.

Rnd 2: Join next color with sc in any ch sp, (4 hdc, sc) in same ch sp, (sc, 4 hdc, sc) in each ch sp around, **do not join**.

Rnd 3: Sk first st, sc in next hdc, *[ch 3, sc in next st] 3 times, sk next 2 sts**, sc in next st, rep from * around, ending last rep at **, join in beg sc.

Rnd 4: Ch 1, sc in first st, ch 5, [working behind sts of last rnd, sk next 4 sts, sc in next st, ch 5] around, join in beg sc. Fasten off.

Rnd 5: Join next color in any ch sp, **ch 3** (*see Pattern Notes*), (2 dc, ch 3, 3 dc) in same ch sp (*corner*), (3 dc, ch 3, 3 dc) in each ch sp around, join in 3rd ch of beg ch-3. Fasten off.

Rnd 6: Join next color in any corner ch sp, ch 3, (2 dc, ch 3, 3 dc) in same ch sp, *ch 1, 3 dc in sp between corner dc groups**, (3 dc, ch 3, 3 dc) in next corner ch sp, rep from * around, ending last rep at **, join in 3rd ch of beg ch-3. Fasten off. ∎

Square 72

FINISHED SIZE
4½ inches square

GAUGE
Rnd 1 = 2 inches in diameter

PATTERN NOTES
Join with slip stitch as indicated unless otherwise stated.

Chain-3 at beginning of row or round counts as first double crochet unless otherwise stated.

Square is made with 3 colors of medium (worsted) weight yarn.

INSTRUCTIONS
SQUARE

Rnd 1 (RS): With size H hook, ch 4, sl st in first ch to form ring, **ch 3** *(see Pattern Notes)*, 2 dc in ring, ch 3, [3 dc in ring, ch 3] 3 times, **join** *(see Pattern Notes)* in 3rd ch of beg ch-3, **turn**. Fasten off.

Rnd 2: Join next color with sc in any ch sp, ch 3, sc in same ch sp *(corner)*, *ch 1, sk next st, sc in next st, ch 1, sk next st**, (sc, ch 3, sc) in next ch sp *(corner)*, rep from * around, ending last rep at **, join in beg sc, turn. Fasten off.

Rnd 3: Working in front of corner ch sp of last rnd, join first color in ch sp on rnd 1 between 2 sc, ch 5 *(counts as first dc and ch-2)*, dc in same ch sp, *[sc in next st on this rnd, working behind ch sp of last rnd, dc in sk st on rnd 1] twice, sc in next st on this rnd**, working in front of ch sp on last rnd, (dc, ch 2, dc) in ch sp on rnd 1 between 2 sc at corner, rep from * around, ending last rep at **, join in 3rd ch of beg ch-5, turn. Fasten off.

Rnd 4: Join next color with sc in any corner ch-2 sp, ch 3, sc in same ch sp, *[ch 1, sk next st, sc in next st] 3 times, ch 1, sk next st**, (sc, ch 3, sc) in next ch sp *(corner)*, rep from * around, ending last rep at **, join in beg sc, turn. Fasten off.

Rnd 5: Working in front of corner ch sp of last rnd, join first color in ch sp on rnd 3 between 2 sc, ch 5 *(counts as first dc and ch-2)*, dc in same ch sp, *[sc in next st on this rnd, working behind ch sp of last rnd, dc in sk st on rnd 3] 4 times, sc in next st on this rnd **, working in front of ch sp on last rnd, (dc, ch 2, dc) in ch sp on rnd 3 between 2 sc, rep from * around, ending last rep at **, join in 3rd ch of beg ch-5, **do not turn**. Fasten off.

Rnd 6: Join 2nd color with sc in any corner ch-2 sp, 2 sc in same ch sp, *[ch 1, sk next st, sc in next st] 5 times, ch 1, sk next st**, 3 sc in next ch sp *(corner)*, rep from * around, ending last rep at **, join in beg sc. Fasten off. ∎

Square 73

FINISHED SIZE
7 inches square

GAUGE
Rnd 1 = 2 inches in diameter

PATTERN NOTES
Join with slip stitch as indicated unless otherwise stated.

Square is made with 1 color of medium (worsted) weight yarn.

SPECIAL STITCH
Cluster (cl): Ch 3 *(counts as first dc)*, holding back last lp of each st on hook, 3 dc in 3rd ch from hook, yo, pull through all lps on hook, ch 1 to close.

INSTRUCTIONS
SQUARE

Rnd 1: With size H hook, ch 4, sl st in first ch to form ring, ch 4 *(counts as first dc and ch-1)*, [dc in ring, ch 1] 11 times, **join** *(see Pattern Notes)* in 3rd ch of beg ch-4.

Rnd 2: Cl *(see Special Stitch)*, *ch 2, cl**, sl st in next st, cl, rep from * around, ending last rep at **, join in joining sl st of rnd 1. Fasten off.

Rnd 3: Join with sc in any ch-2 sp, ch 3, [sc in next ch-2 sp, ch 3] around, join in beg sc.

Rnd 4: Ch 4 *(counts as first tr)*, (tr, {ch 1, tr} 3 times) in same st, *[ch 5, sc in next ch sp] 3 times, ch 5** (tr, {ch 1, tr} 4 times) in next st, rep from * around, ending last rep at **, join in 4th ch of beg ch-4.

Rnd 5: Sl st across to next st, ch 1, sc in same st, *ch 5, sk next st, sc in next st, [ch 5, sc in next ch sp] 4 times, ch 5, sk next st**, sc in next st, rep from * around, ending last rep at **, join in beg sc.

Rnd 6: Sl st in first ch sp, ch 3 *(counts as first dc)*, (2 dc, ch 3, 3 dc) in same ch sp, *[ch 1, 3 dc in next ch sp] 5 times, ch 1**, (3 dc, ch 3, 3 dc) in next ch sp, join in 3rd ch of beg ch-3. Fasten off. ∎

Square 74

FINISHED SIZE
5 inches square

GAUGE
Rnds 1 & 2 = 2 inches in diameter

PATTERN NOTES
Chain-3 at beginning of row or round counts as first double crochet unless otherwise stated.

Join with slip stitch as indicated unless otherwise stated.

Square is made with 1 color of medium (worsted) weight yarn.

INSTRUCTIONS
SQUARE
Rnd 1: With size H hook, ch 4, sl st in first ch to form ring, ch 6 *(counts as first dc and ch-3)*, [3 dc in ring, ch 3] 3 times, 2 dc in ring, **join** *(see Pattern Notes)* in 3rd ch of beg ch-6.

Rnd 2: Sl st in first ch sp, ch 1, (sc, ch 3, sc) in same ch sp, *sc in each of next 3 sts**, (sc, ch 3, sc) in next ch sp, rep from * around, ending last rep at **, join in beg sc.

Rnd 3: Sl st in first ch sp, **ch 3** *(see Pattern Notes)*, (dc, ch 3, 2 dc) in same ch sp, *sk next st, dc in each of next 3 sts, sk next st**, (2 dc, ch 3, 2 dc) in next ch sp, rep from * around, ending last rep at **, join in 3rd ch of beg ch-3.

Rnd 4: Sl st in next st, ch 1, (2 sc, ch 3, 2 sc) in next ch sp, *sc in each of next 3 sts, ch 7, sl st in next st, ch 2, (dc, 2 hdc, sc, ch 1) in ch-7 sp just formed, **fpsl st** *(see Stitch Guide)* around center dc of dc group on rnd 1 below, (ch 1, sc, 2 hdc, dc, ch 2) in same ch-7 sp, sl st in same st as last sl st on this rnd, sc in each of next 3 sts**, (2 sc, ch 3, 2 sc) in next ch sp, rep from * around, ending last rep at **, join in beg sc.

Rnd 5: Sl st in next st, ch 1, (sc, ch 3, sc) in next ch sp, *sk next st, sc in each of next 9 sts, sk next st**, (sc, ch 3, sc) in next ch sp, rep from * around, ending last rep at **, join in beg sc.

Rnd 6: Sl st in first ch sp, ch 4 *(counts as first dc and ch-1)*, (dc, {ch 1, dc} 3 times) in same ch sp, *[ch 1, sk next st, dc in next st] 5 times, ch 1, sk next st**, (dc, {ch 1, dc} 4 times) in next ch sp, rep from * around, ending last rep at **, join in 3rd ch of beg ch-3. Fasten off. ∎

Square 75

FINISHED SIZE
7 inches square

GAUGE
Rnd 1 = 1½ inches in diameter

PATTERN NOTES
Join with slip stitch as indicated unless otherwise stated.

Chain-3 at beginning of row or round counts as first double crochet unless otherwise stated.

Square is made with 4 colors of medium (worsted) weight yarn, 1 of which is variegated.

INSTRUCTIONS
SQUARE
Rnd 1: With size H hook, ch 4, 11 dc in 4th ch from hook *(first 3 chs counts as first dc)*, **join** *(see Pattern Notes)* in 3rd ch of beg ch-3.

Rnd 2: Ch 1, sc in first st, ch 5, sk next 2 sts, [sc in next st, ch 5, sk next 2 sts] around, join in beg sc.

Rnd 3: Sl st in first ch sp, **ch 3** *(see Pattern Notes)*, 5 dc in same ch sp, ch 1, [6 dc in next ch sp, ch 1] around, join in 3rd ch of beg ch-3. Fasten off.

Rnd 4: Join next color with sc in any ch sp, *ch 6, sk next 3 sts, sc in sp before next st, ch 6**, sc in next ch sp, rep from * around, ending last rep at **, join in beg sc.

Rnd 5: Sl st in first ch sp, ch 3, (3 dc, ch 2, 4 dc) in same ch sp *(corner)*, *dc in next ch sp, **fptr** *(see Stitch Guide)* around 2nd dc between sc of last rnd, dc in same ch sp on this rnd**, (4 dc, ch 2, 4 dc) in next ch sp *(corner)*, rep from * around, ending last rep at **, join in 3rd ch of beg ch-3. Fasten off.

Rnd 6: Join first color in any corner ch sp, ch 3, 4 dc in same ch sp, *dc in each of next 5 sts, fptr around fptr, sk st behind fptr on this rnd, dc in each of next 5 sts**, 5 dc in next corner ch sp, rep from * around, ending last rep at **, join in 3rd ch of beg ch-3. Fasten off.

Rnd 7: Working in **back lps** *(see Stitch Guide)*, join next color in any center corner st, ch 3, (2 dc, ch 2, 3 dc) in same st, *dc in each of next 7 sts, fptr around next fptr, sk st behind fptr on this rnd, dc in each of next 7 sts**, (3 dc, ch 2, 3 dc) in next st, rep from * around, ending last rep at **, join in 3rd ch of beg ch-3. Fasten off. ∎

Square 76

FINISHED SIZE
6½ inches square

GAUGE
Rnds 1–3 = 4 inches in diameter

PATTERN NOTES
Join with slip stitch as indicated unless otherwise stated.

Chain-3 at beginning of row or round counts as first double crochet unless otherwise stated.

Square is made with 4 colors of medium (worsted) weight yarn.

INSTRUCTIONS
SQUARE
Rnd 1: With size H hook, ch 4, sl st in first ch to form ring, [sl st in ring, ch 8] 6 times, **join** (see Pattern Notes) in beg sl st. Fasten off.

Rnd 2: Working ring behind ch sps, join next color with sc in ring between sl sts, ch 5, [sc in ring between next 2 sl sts, ch 5] around, join in beg sc.

Rnd 3: Sl st in first ch-5 sp, (sc, hdc, 5 dc, hdc, sc) in same ch sp (petal) and in each ch sp around, join in beg sc.

Rnd 4: Ch 1, sc in first st, ch 3, sk next st, [sc in next st, ch 3, sk next st] around, join in beg sc. Fasten off.

Rnd 5: Working behind petals, join next color with **bpsc** (see Stitch Guide) around sc on rnd 2, ch 5, [bpsc around next sc on rnd 2, ch 5] around, join in beg bpsc.

Rnd 6: Sl st in first ch sp, **ch 3** (see Pattern Notes), (2 dc, ch 1, 3 dc) in same ch sp, [ch 1, (3 dc, ch 1, 3 dc) in next ch sp] around, join with sc in 3rd ch of beg ch-3 forming last ch sp.

Rnd 7: Ch 3, 2 dc in last ch sp, *3 dc in each of next 2 ch sps**, (3 dc, ch 3, 3 dc) in next ch sp (corner), rep from * around, ending last rep at **, 3 dc in same ch sp as beg ch-3, ch 1, join with hdc in 3rd ch of beg ch-3 forming last ch sp.

Rnd 8: Ch 3, 2 dc in last ch sp, *ch 1, [3 dc in next ch sp, ch 1] 3 times**, (3 dc, ch 3, 3 dc) in next corner ch sp, rep from * around, ending last rep at **, 3 dc in same ch sp as beg ch-3, ch 3, join in 3rd ch of beg ch-3. Fasten off.

Rnd 9: Join next color in any corner ch sp, ch 3, (2 dc, ch 3, 3 dc) in same ch sp, *3 dc in each of next 4 ch sps**, (3 dc, ch 3, 3 dc) in next corner ch sp, rep from * around, ending last rep at **, join in 3rd ch of beg ch-3. Fasten off. ∎

Square 77

FINISHED SIZE
7 inches square

GAUGE
Rnds 1 & 2 = 2½ inches in diameter

PATTERN NOTES
Join with slip stitch as indicated unless otherwise stated.

Chain-3 at beginning of row or round counts as first double crochet unless otherwise stated.

Square is made with 3 colors of medium (worsted) weight yarn.

INSTRUCTIONS
SQUARE
Rnd 1: With size H hook, ch 4, sl st in first ch to form ring, **ch 3** (see Pattern Notes), 11 dc in ring, **join** (see Pattern Notes) in 3rd ch of beg ch-3.

Rnd 2: Ch 3, dc in same st, 2 dc in next st, *ch 1, sk next st**, 2 dc in each of next 2 sts, rep from * around, ending last rep at **, join in 3rd ch of beg ch-3. Fasten off.

Rnd 3: Join next color with sc in first st, *ch 7, sc in 2nd ch from hook, hdc in each of next 2 chs, dc in each of next 2 chs, tr in last ch (petal), sk next 2 sts, sc in next st, ch 1, sk next ch sp**, sc in next st, rep from * around, ending last rep at **, join in beg sc. Fasten off.

Rnd 4: Join next color with sc in first sc at tip of any petal, 2 sc in same st, *sc in each of next 5 sts on petal, sc in next st, working over ch-1 sp on last rnd, sc in ch-1 sp on rnd 2, tr in sk st on rnd 1, sc in ch sp on rnd 2, sc in next st, working on opposite side of ch-7, sc in each of next 5 chs**, 3 sc in tip of petal, rep from * around, ending last rep at **, join in beg sc.

Rnd 5: Ch 1, sc in first st, *3 sc in next st, sc in each of next 6 sts, sk next st, sc in each of next 3 sts, sk next st**, sc in each of next 6 sts, rep from * around, ending last rep at **, sc in each st around, join in beg sc. Fasten off.

Rnd 6: Join 2nd color with sc in center st at tip of petal, 2 sc in same st, *sc in each of next 3 sts, hdc in each of next 3 sts, sk next 2 sts, 5 dc in next st, sk next 2 sts, hdc in each of next 3 sts, sc in each of next 3 sts**, 3 sc in next st, rep from * around, ending last rep at **, join in beg sc. Fasten off.

Rnd 7: Join first color in first st, ch 6 (counts as first dc and ch-3), *sk next st, dc in both lps of next st, dc in back lps (see Stitch Guide) of each of next 6 sts, **fpdc** (see Stitch Guide) around each of next 5 sts**, dc in back lps of each of next 6 sts, dc in both lps of next st, ch 3, rep from * around, ending last rep at **, dc in each st around, join in 3rd ch of beg ch-3. Fasten off.

Rnd 8: Join 3rd color with sc in any ch sp, 4 sc in same ch sp, sc in each st around with 5 sc in each ch sp, join in beg sc. Fasten off. ■

Square 78

FINISHED SIZE
5 inches square

GAUGE
Rnds 1 & 2 = 3 inches in diameter

PATTERN NOTES
Chain-3 at beginning of row or round counts as first
  double crochet unless otherwise stated.

Join with slip stitch as indicated unless otherwise
  stated.

Square is made with 2 colors of medium (worsted)
  weight yarn.

INSTRUCTIONS
SQUARE
Rnd 1: With size H hook, ch 2, 12 sc in 2nd ch
  from hook, **join** (*see Pattern Notes*) in beg sc.

Rnd 2: Ch 3 (*see Pattern Notes*), dc in each of
  next 2 sts, ch 3, [dc in each of next 3 sts, ch 3]
  around, join in 3rd ch of beg ch-3.

Rnd 3: Ch 3, dc in each of next 2 sts, *(3 dc, ch 3,
  3 dc) in next ch sp (*corner*)**, dc in each of next
  3 sts, rep from * around, ending last rep at **,
  join in 3rd ch of beg ch-3. Fasten off.

Rnd 4: Working in **back lps** (*see Stitch Guide*),
  join next color with sc in any corner ch sp, (sc,
  ch 2, 2 sc) in same ch sp, *sc in each of next 2
  sts, **fptr** (*see Stitch Guide*) around next dc on
  rnd 2, sk st behind fptr on this rnd, sc in next st,
  sk next st on rnd 2, fptr around next st on rnd 2,
  sk st behind fptr on this rnd, sc in each of next
  2 sts**, (2 sc, ch 2, 2 sc) in next ch sp, rep from
  * around, ending last rep at **, join in beg sc.
  Fasten off.

Rnd 5: Join first color in any corner ch sp, ch 3,
  (dc, ch 3, 2 dc) in same ch sp, *working in back
  lps, sk next st, dc in each of next 9 sts, sk next
  st**, (2 dc, ch 3, 2 dc) in next corner ch sp, rep
  from * around, ending last rep at **, join in 3rd
  ch of beg ch-3. Fasten off.

Rnd 6: Join 2nd color with sc in any corner ch sp,
  2 sc in same ch sp, *fptr around sc in rnd 4, sk
  st behind fptr on this rnd, working in back lps,
  sc in each of next 5 sts, fptr around sc between
  fptr on rnd 4, sk st behind fptr on this rnd, sc
  in each of next 5 sts, fptr around 2nd st of next
  corner on rnd 4, sk st behind fptr on this rnd**,
  3 sc in next corner ch sp, rep from * around,
  ending last rep at **, join in beg sc. Fasten off. ∎

Square 79

FINISHED SIZE
6 inches square

GAUGE
Rnds 1–4 = 5 inches in diameter

PATTERN NOTES
Join with slip stitch as indicated unless otherwise stated.

Chain-3 at beginning of row or round counts as first double crochet unless otherwise stated.

Square is made with 2 colors of medium (worsted) weight yarn.

SPECIAL STITCH
Front post cluster (fpcl): Holding back last lp of each st on hook 3 **fptr** (*see Stitch Guide*) around place indicated, yo, pull through all lps on hook.

INSTRUCTIONS
SQUARE
Rnd 1: With size H hook, ch 5, 23 tr in 5th ch from hook (*first 4 chs count as first tr*), **join** (*see Pattern Notes*) in 4th ch of beg ch-4.

Rnd 2: **Bpdc** (*see Stitch Guide*) around first st, 2 **fpdc** (*see Stitch Guide*) around next st, [bpdc around next st, 2 fpdc around next st] around, join in beg bpdc.

Rnd 3: Bpdc around first bpdc, *fpdc around next fpdc, dc in sp between this st and next st, fpdc around next fpdc**, bpdc around next bpdc, rep from * around, ending last rep at **, join in beg bpdc.

Rnd 4: **Bpsl st** (*see Stitch Guide*) around first st, ch 5, *sk next fpdc, **fpcl** (*see Special Stitch*) around next dc, ch 2, sk next fpdc**, bpdc around next bpdc, ch 2, rep from * around, ending last rep at **, join in 3rd ch of beg ch-5. Fasten off.

Rnd 5: Join next color in first ch sp, **ch 3** (*see Pattern Notes*), 3 dc in same ch sp, *2 dc in each of next 4 ch sps, 4 dc in next ch sp, ch 3**, 4 dc in next ch sp, rep from * around, ending last rep at **, join in 3rd ch of beg ch-3. Fasten off.

Rnd 6: Join first color with sc in any ch sp, 2 sc in same ch sp, sc in each st around with 3 sc in each ch sp, join in beg sc. Fasten off. ■

Square 80

FINISHED SIZE
7¼ inches square

GAUGE
Rnds 1–4 = 4 inches in diameter

PATTERN NOTES
Join with slip stitch as indicated unless otherwise stated.

Chain-3 at beginning of row or round counts as first double crochet unless otherwise stated.

Square is made with 2 colors of medium (worsted) weight yarn.

INSTRUCTIONS
SQUARE
Rnd 1: With size H hook, ch 5, sl st in first ch to form ring, ch 1, [3 sc in ring, ch 3] 4 rimes, **join** (*see Pattern Notes*) in beg sc.

Rnd 2: Ch 1, sc in each of first 3 sts, (sc, ch 10, sc) in next ch sp, sc in each st around with (sc, ch 10, sc) in each ch sp, join in beg sc. Fasten off.

Rnd 3: Join next color in any ch-3 sp on rnd 1 behind ch-10, **ch 3** *(see Pattern Notes)*, (dc, ch 2, 2 dc) in same ch sp, *sk next st, dc in each of next 3 sts on this rnd, sk next st**, (2 dc, ch 2, 2 dc) in next ch-3 sp on rnd 1 behind ch-10, rep from * around, ending last rep at **, join in 3rd ch of beg ch-3.

Rnd 4: Ch 3, dc in next st, *2 dc in next ch sp, (dc, ch 8, sl st in top of last dc, dc) in ch-10 sp on rnd 2, 2 dc in same ch sp on this rnd**, dc in each of next 7 sts, rep from * around, ending last rep at **, dc in each st around, join in 3rd ch of beg ch-3. Fasten off.

Rnd 5: Join first color in dc after any ch-8, ch 3, dc in each of next 4 sts, *fptr *(see Stitch Guide)* around each of next 3 sts on rnd 3, sk 3 sts behind fptr on this rnd, dc in each of next 5 sts, ch 5, working behind ch sp, sk next ch-8 sp**, dc in each of next 5 sts, rep from * around, ending last rep at **, join in 3rd ch of beg ch-3.

Rnd 6: Ch 3, dc in each of next 4 sts, *fpdc *(see Stitch Guide)* around each of next 3 fptr, dc in each of next 5 sts, 2 dc in next ch sp, working in front of ch sp on last rnd, (dc, ch 8, sl st in top of last dc, dc) in next ch-8 sp on rnd 4, 2 dc in same ch sp on this rnd**, dc in each of next 5 sts, rep from * around, ending last rep at **, join in 3rd ch of beg ch-3. Fasten off.

Rnd 7: Join 2nd color in dc after any ch-8, ch 3, dc in each st around with ch 5 at each corner, join in 3rd ch of beg ch-3.

Rnd 8: Ch 1, sc in each st around with 3 sc in each ch-8 sp in front of ch-5 sp of last rnd on rnd 6, join in beg sc. Fasten off. ■

Square 81

FINISHED SIZE
7½ inches square

GAUGE
Rnds 1–3 = 3¾ inches

PATTERN NOTES
Join with slip stitch as indicated unless otherwise stated.

Chain-3 at beginning of row or round counts as first double crochet unless otherwise stated.

Square is made with 4 colors of medium (worsted) weight yarn.

SPECIAL STITCHES
Beginning cluster (beg cl): Ch 3 *(counts as first dc)*, holding back last lp of each st on hook, 2 dc in place indicated, yo, pull through all lps on hook.

Cluster (cl): Holding back last lp of each st on hook, 3 dc in place indicated, yo, pull through all lps on hook.

INSTRUCTIONS
SQUARE
Rnd 1: With size H hook, ch 4, sl st in first ch to form ring, ch 5 *(counts as first dc and ch-2)*, [dc

in ring, ch 2] 7 times, **join** *(see Pattern Notes)* in 3rd ch of beg ch-5. Fasten off.

Rnd 2: Join next color in any ch sp, **beg cl** *(see Special Stitches)* in same ch sp, ch 4, [**cl** *(see Special Stitches)* in next ch sp, ch 4] around, join in beg cl. Fasten off.

Rnd 3: Join next color with sc in any ch sp, 5 sc in same ch sp, 6 sc in each ch sp around, join in beg sc.

Rnd 4: Working in **back lps** *(see Stitch Guide)*, ch 5, sk next st, [dc in next st, ch 2, sk next st] around, join in 3rd ch of beg ch-5. Fasten off.

Rnd 5: Join next color with sc in any ch sp, ch 4, [sc in next ch sp, ch 4] around, join in beg sc.

Rnd 6: Sl st in first ch sp, ch 5 *(counts as first tr and ch-1)*, (tr, {ch 1, tr} 3 times) in same ch sp *(corner)*, *[ch 2, dc in next ch sp] 5 times, ch 2**, (tr, {ch 1, tr} 4 times) in next ch sp *(corner)*, rep from * around, ending last rep at **, join in 4th ch of beg ch-5.

Rnd 7: Sl st in first ch sp, **ch 3** *(see Pattern Notes)*, dc in same ch sp, ch 1, *2 dc in next ch sp, ch 4**, [2 dc in next ch sp, ch 1] 9 times, rep from * around, ending last rep at **, [2 dc in next ch sp, ch 1] around, join in 3rd ch of beg ch-3. Fasten off. ∎

Square 82

FINISHED SIZE
6½ inches square

GAUGE
Rnds 1 & 2 = 2¼ inches in diameter

PATTERN NOTES
Join with slip stitch as indicated unless otherwise stated.

Chain-3 at beginning of row or round counts as first double crochet unless otherwise stated.

Square is made with 4 colors of medium (worsted) weight yarn.

INSTRUCTIONS
SQUARE

Rnd 1: With size H hook, ch 2, 12 sc in 2nd ch from hook, **join** *(see Pattern Notes)* in beg sc. Fasten off.

Rnd 2: Join next color in any st, **ch 3** *(see Pattern Notes)*, dc in same st, 2 dc in each st around, join in 3rd ch of beg ch-3. Fasten off.

Rnd 3: Join next color with sc in any st, **fpdc** *(see Stitch Guide)* around next st, [sc in next st, fpdc around next st] around, join in beg sc.

Rnd 4: Ch 3, dc in same st, fpdc around next fpdc, [2 dc in next st, fpdc around next fpdc] around, join in 3rd ch of beg ch-3.

Rnd 5: Ch 3, dc in next st, 2 fpdc around next st, [dc in each of next 2 sts, 2 fpdc around next st] around, join in 3rd ch of beg ch-3. Fasten off.

Rnd 6: Join next color in first st, ch 4 *(counts as first dc and ch-1)*, dc in next st, [fpdc around each of next 2 fpdc, dc in next st, ch 1, dc in next st] 11 times, fpdc around each of next 2 fpdc, join in 3rd ch of beg ch-4. Fasten off.

Rnd 7: Join 2nd color in any ch sp, ch 3, (dc, ch 2, 2 dc) in same ch sp, *sk next 2 sts, hdc in each of next 2 sts, sc in next ch sp, sc in each of next 4 sts, hdc in each of next 2 sts, sc in next ch sp, sk next 2 sts**, (2 dc, ch 2, 2 dc) in next ch sp, rep from * around, ending last rep at **, join in 3rd ch of beg ch-3. Fasten off.

Rnd 8: Join first color in any ch sp, ch 3, (dc, ch 2, 2 dc) in same ch sp, *sk next st, sc in each of next 12 sts, sk next st**, (2 dc, ch 2, 2 dc) in next ch sp, rep from * around, ending last rep at **, join in 3rd ch of beg ch-3. Fasten off. ■

Square 83

FINISHED SIZE
8 inches square

GAUGE
Rnd 1 = 2 inches in diameter

PATTERN NOTES
Join with slip stitch as indicated unless otherwise stated.

Chain-3 at beginning of row or round counts as first double crochet unless otherwise stated.

Square made with 1 color of medium (worsted) weight yarn.

SPECIAL STITCH
Picot: Ch 4, sl st in 4th ch from hook.

INSTRUCTIONS
SQUARE
Rnd 1: With Size H hook, ch 5, sl st in first ch to form ring, ch 4 *(counts as first dc and ch-1)*, [dc in ring, ch 1] 7 times, **join** *(see Pattern Notes)* in 3rd ch of beg ch-4.

Rnd 2: Ch 1, sc in first st, *sc in next ch sp, **picot** *(see Special Stitch)***, sc in next st, rep from * around, ending last rep at **, join in beg sc.

Rnd 3: Sl st in next st, ch 1, sc in same st, *ch 8, sk next picot and next st, sc in next st, rep from * around, ch 4, join with tr in beg sc forming last ch sp.

Rnd 4: Ch 1, sc in this ch sp, ch 6, [sc in next ch sp, ch 6] around, join in beg sc.

Rnd 5: Ch 1, sc in first st, 6 sc in next ch sp, [sc in next st, 6 sc in next ch sp] around, join in beg sc.

Rnd 6: Ch 1, sc in each st around, join in beg sc.

Rnd 7: Ch 1, sc in first st, [ch 3, sk next st, sc in next st] around, ch 1, sk last st, hdc in beg sc forming last ch sp.

Rnd 8: Ch 1, sc in this ch sp, [ch 5, sc in next ch sp] around, ch 2, join with dc in beg sc forming last ch sp.

Rnd 9: Ch 1, sc in this ch sp, *[ch 3, sc in next ch sp] 5 times, ch 2, (tr, {ch 2, tr} 3 times) in next ch sp, ch 2**, sc in next ch sp, rep from * around, ending last rep at **, join in beg sc.

Rnd 10: Ch 1, sc in first st, [sc in next ch sp, sc in next st] 7 times, *3 sc in next ch sp, sc in next st**, [sc in next ch sp, sc in next st] 9 times, rep from * around, ending last rep at **, sc in next ch sp, sc in next st, sc in last ch sp, join in beg sc. Fasten off. ■

Square 84

FINISHED SIZE
9 inches square

GAUGE
Rnd 1 = 1½ inches in diameter

PATTERN NOTES
Join with slip stitch as indicated unless otherwise stated.

Chain-3 at beginning of row or round counts as first double crochet unless otherwise stated.

Square is made with 3 colors of medium (worsted) weight yarn.

SPECIAL STITCH
Popcorn (pc): 4 dc in place indicated, drop lp from hook, insert hook in first dc of group, pull dropped lp through, ch 1 to secure.

INSTRUCTIONS
SQUARE
Rnd 1: With size H hook, ch 5, sl st in first ch to form ring, **ch 3** *(see Pattern Notes)*, 11 dc in ring, **join** *(see Pattern Notes)* in 3rd ch of beg ch-3.

Rnd 2: Ch 1, 3 sc in first st, **pc** *(see Special Stitch)* in next st, [3 sc in next st, pc in next st] around, join in beg sc.

Rnd 3: Ch 1, sc in first st and in each st around, join in beg sc.

Rnd 4: Ch 1, 2 sc in first st, *pc in next st, 2 sc in next st, sc in next st**, 2 sc in next st, rep from * around, ending last rep at **, sc in last st, join in beg sc.

Rnd 5: Ch 1, sc in each of first 2 sts, 2 sc in next st, [sc in each of next 2 sts, 2 sc in next st] around, join in beg sc. Fasten off.

Rnd 6: Join next color with sc in any st, sc in each of next 2 sts, *ch 6, sl st in 2nd ch from hook *(tip)*, sc in each of next 4 chs *(petal)***, sc in each of next 4 sts, rep from * around, ending last rep at **, sc in last st, join in beg sc.

Rnd 7: Ch 1, sc in each of first 2 sts, *ch 3, sk next st, working on opposite side of ch-6, sk first ch, dc in next ch, hdc in next ch, sc in next ch, (sl st, ch 2, sl st) in tip, sc in next st, hdc in next st, dc in next st, ch 3, sk next 2 sts**, sc in each of next 2 sts, rep from * around, ending last rep at **, join in beg sc. Fasten off.

Rnd 8: Join next color with sc in any ch sp at tip, sc in same ch sp, *working in **back lps** *(see Stitch Guide)*, sk next sl st, hdc in next st, dc in next st, **tr dec** *(see Stitch Guide)* in last st on this petal and first st on next petal, dc in next st, hdc in next st**, 2 sc in next ch-2 sp at tip of this petal, rep from * around, ending last rep at **, join in beg sc.

Rnd 9: Ch 5 *(counts as first dtr)*, 2 dtr in same st, *3 dtr in next st, sk next 2 sts, 3 tr in next st, sk next 2 sts, 3 dc in next st, [sk next 2 sts, 3 hdc in next st] twice, sk next 2 sts, 3 dc in next st, sk next 2 sts, 3 tr in next st, sk next st**, 3 dtr in next st, rep from * around, ending last rep at **, join in 5th ch of beg ch-5. Fasten off. ∎

Square 85

FINISHED SIZE
7 inches square

GAUGE
Rnd 1 = 1½ inches in diameter

PATTERN NOTES
Join with slip stitch as indicated unless otherwise stated.

Chain-3 at beginning of row or round counts as first double crochet unless otherwise stated.

Square is made with 1 color of medium (worsted) weight yarn.

INSTRUCTIONS
SQUARE
Rnd 1: With size H hook, ch 4, sl st in first ch to form ring, **ch 3** (see Pattern Notes), 11 dc in ring, **join** (see Pattern Notes) in 3rd ch of beg ch-3.

Rnd 2: Ch 3, (dc, ch 3, 2 dc) in same st, *dc in each of next 2 sts**, (2 dc, ch 3, 2 dc) in next st, rep from * around, ending last rep at **, join in 3rd ch of beg ch-3.

Rnd 3: Sl st in next st and next ch sp, ch 3, (dc, ch 3, 2 dc) in same ch sp, *fpdc (see Stitch Guide) around each of next 2 sts, dc in each of next 2 sts, fpdc around each of next 2 sts**, (2 dc, ch 3, 2 dc) in next ch sp, rep from * around, ending last rep at **, join in 3rd ch of beg ch-3.

Rnd 4: Ch 3, dc in next st, *(2 dc, ch 3, 2 dc) in next ch sp, dc in each of next 2 sts, fpdc around each of next 2 fpdc, dc in each of next 2 sts, fpdc around each of next 2 fpdc**, dc in each of next 2 sts, rep from * around, ending last rep at **, join in 3rd ch of beg ch-3.

Rnd 5: Ch 3, dc in each of next 3 sts, *(2 dc, ch 3, 2 dc) in next ch sp, dc in each of next 4 sts, fpdc around each of next 2 fpdc, dc in each of next 2 sts, fpdc around each of next 2 fpdc**, dc in each of next 4 sts, rep from * around, ending last rep at **, join in 3rd ch of beg ch-3.

Rnd 6: Ch 3, dc in each of next 5 sts, *(2 dc, ch 3, 2 dc) in next ch sp, dc in each of next 6 sts, fpdc around each of next 2 fpdc, dc in each of next 2 sts, fpdc around each of next 2 fpdc**, dc in each of next 6 sts, rep from * around, ending last rep at **, join in 3rd ch of beg ch-3. Fasten off. ∎

Square 86

FINISHED SIZE
7½ inches square

GAUGE
Rnds 1 & 2 = 3 inches in diameter

PATTERN NOTES
Join with slip stitch as indicated unless otherwise stated.

Chain-3 at beginning of row or round counts as first double crochet unless otherwise stated.

Square is made with 3 colors of medium (worsted) weight yarn.

INSTRUCTIONS
SQUARE
Rnd 1: With size H hook, ch 4, 15 dc in 4th ch from hook (*first 3 chs count as first dc*), **join** (*see Pattern Notes*) in 3rd ch of beg ch-3.

Rnd 2: Ch 5 (*counts as first hdc and ch-3*), sk next st, [hdc in next st, ch 3, sk next st] around, join in 2nd ch of beg ch-5. Fasten off.

Rnd 3: Join next color with sc in any ch sp, (hdc, 2 dc, hdc, sc) in same ch sp, (sc, hdc, 2 dc, hdc, sc) in each ch sp around, join in beg sc. Fasten off.

Rnd 4: Join next color with sc in sp between any 2 dc, *ch 6, sc in sp between next 2 dc, ch 2, (dc, ch 2, tr, ch 2, dc) in sp between next 2 sc, ch 2**, sc in sp between next 2 dc, rep from * around, ending last rep at **, join in beg sc.

Rnd 5: Sl st in first ch sp, **ch 3** (*see Pattern Notes*), 4 dc in same ch sp, *2 dc in next ch sp, dc in next st, 2 dc in next ch sp, (dc, ch 3, dc) in next st (*corner*), 2 dc in next ch sp, dc in next st, 2 dc in next ch sp**, 5 dc in next ch sp, rep from * around, ending last rep at **, join in 3rd ch of beg ch-3. Fasten off.

Rnd 6: Join first color with sc in any corner ch sp, *[ch 4, sk next 2 sts, sc in next st] 5 times, ch 4, sk next 2 sts**, (sc, ch 7, sc) in next corner ch sp, rep from * around, ending last rep at **, sc in same ch sp as beg sc, ch 7, join in beg sc.

Rnd 7: Sl st in first ch sp, ch 1, (2 sc, ch 1, 2 sc) in same ch sp and in each of next 5 ch sps, *(4 sc, ch 1, 4 sc) in corner ch sp**, (2 sc, ch 1, 2 sc) in each of next 6 ch sps, rep from * around, ending last rep at **, join in beg sc. Fasten off. ∎

Square 87

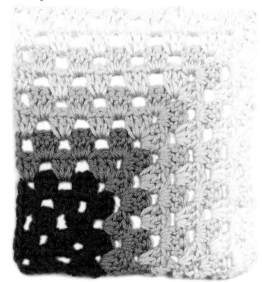

FINISHED SIZE
6¾ inches square

GAUGE
Rnds 1 & 2 = 2½ inches in diameter

PATTERN NOTES
Join with slip stitch as indicated unless otherwise stated.

Chain-3 at beginning of row or round counts as first double crochet unless otherwise stated.

Square is made with 5 colors of medium (worsted) weight yarn.

INSTRUCTIONS
SQUARE
Rnd 1: With size H hook, ch 4, sl st in first ch to form ring, **ch 3** (*see Pattern Notes*), 2 dc in ring, [ch 2, 3 dc in ring] 3 times, join with hdc in 3rd ch of beg ch-3 forming last ch sp.

Rnd 2: Ch 3, (2 dc, ch 2, 3 dc) in this ch sp, ch 1, [(3 dc, ch 2, 3 dc) in next ch sp, ch 1] around, **join** (see Pattern Notes) in 3rd ch of beg ch-3. Fasten off.

Row 3: Now working in rows, join next color in any ch-2 sp, ch 3, 2 dc in same ch sp, ch 1, 3 dc in next ch-1 sp, ch 1, (3 dc, ch 2, 3 dc) in next ch-2 sp, [ch 1, 3 dc in next ch sp] twice, leaving rem sts unworked, turn.

Row 4: Ch 4 (counts as first dc and ch-1), [3 dc in next ch sp, ch 1] twice, (3 dc, ch 2, 3 dc) in next ch sp, [ch 1, 3 dc in next ch sp] twice, ch 1, dc in last st, turn. Fasten off.

Row 5: Join next color in first st, ch 3, 2 dc in next ch sp, [ch 1, 3 dc in next ch sp] twice, (3 dc, ch 2, 3 dc) in next ch sp, [ch 1, 3 dc in next ch sp] 3 times, turn.

Row 6: Ch 4, [3 dc in next ch sp, ch 1] 3 times, (3 dc, ch 2, 3 dc) in next ch sp, [ch 1, 3 dc in next ch sp] 3 times, ch 1, dc in last st, turn. Fasten off.

Row 7: Join next color in first st, ch 3, 2 dc in next ch sp, [ch 1, 3 dc in next ch sp] 3 times, ch 1, (3 dc, ch 2, 3 dc) in next ch sp, [ch 1, 3 dc in next ch sp] 4 times, turn.

Row 8: Ch 4, [3 dc in next ch sp, ch 1] 4 times, (3 dc, ch 2, 3 dc) in next ch sp, [ch 1, 3 dc in next ch sp] 5 times, turn. Fasten off.

Row 9: Join next color in first st, ch 4, [3 dc in next ch sp, ch 1] 5 times, (3 dc, ch 2, 3 dc) in next ch sp, [ch 1, 3 dc in next ch sp] 5 times, turn.

Row 10: Ch 4, [3 dc in next ch sp, ch 1] 5 times, (3 dc, ch 2, 3 dc) in next ch sp, [ch 1, 3 dc in next ch sp] 6 times. Fasten off. ■

Square 88

FINISHED SIZE
6¾ inches square

GAUGE
Rnds 1 & 2 = 3¼ inches in diameter

PATTERN NOTES
Join with slip stitch as indicated unless otherwise stated.

Chain-3 at beginning of row or round counts as first double crochet unless otherwise stated.

Square is made with 4 colors of medium (worsted) weight yarn.

INSTRUCTIONS
SQUARE
Rnd 1: With size H hook, ch 4, sl st in first ch to form ring, ch 5 (counts as first dc and ch-2), [dc in ring, ch 2] 7 times, **join** (see Pattern Notes) in 3rd ch of beg ch-5.

Rnd 2: Sl st in first ch sp, **ch 3** (see Pattern Notes), 3 dc in same ch sp, *ch 2, sk next st**, 4 dc in next ch sp, rep from * around, ending last rep at **, join in 3rd ch of beg ch-3. Fasten off.

Rnd 3: Join next color with sc in first dc of any dc group, sc in each of next 3 dc, *working over ch sp of last rnd, dc in sk st on rnd 1**, sc in each of next 4 sts, rep from * around, ending last rep at **, join in beg sc. Fasten off.

Rnd 4: Working in **back lps** (*see Stitch Guide*), sk first 4 sts, join next color in back lp of next st, ch 3, 4 dc in same st, *sk next 4 sts, (3 dc, ch 2, 3 dc) in next st (*corner*), sk next 4 sts**, 5 dc in next st, rep from * around, ending last rep at **, join in 3rd ch of beg ch-3. Fasten off.

Rnd 5: Join next color in any corner ch sp, ch 3, (dc, ch 2, 2 dc) in same ch sp, dc in each st around, with (2 dc, ch 2, 2 dc) in each corner ch sp, join in 3rd ch of beg ch-3.

Rnd 6: Join 2nd color with sc in any ch sp, 2 sc in same ch sp, sc in each st around with 3 sc in each ch sp, join in beg sc. Fasten off.

Rnd 7: Join first color with sc in any center corner st, 2 sc in same st, *ch 2, sk next st, [sc in next st, ch 1, sk next st] 7 times, ch 2, sc in next st, sk next st**, 3 sc in next st, rep from * around, ending last rep at **, join in beg sc. Fasten off. ■

Square 89

FINISHED SIZE
8¾ inches square

GAUGE
Rnd 1 = 1½ inches in diameter

PATTERN NOTES
Join with slip stitch as indicated unless otherwise stated.

Chain-3 at beginning of row or round counts as first double crochet unless otherwise stated.

Square is made with 4 colors of medium (worsted) weight yarn.

INSTRUCTIONS
SQUARE
Rnd 1: With size H hook, ch 4, sl st in first ch to form ring, **ch 3** (*see Pattern Notes*), 17 dc in ring, **join** (*see Pattern Notes*) in 3rd ch of beg ch-3. Fasten off.

Row 2: Now working in rows, join next color with sc in any st, ch 10, hdc in 2nd ch from hook, hdc in each of next 2 chs, sc in each of next 3 chs, sl st in each of last 3 chs, sl st in same st on rnd 1, leaving rem sts unworked, turn.

Row 3: Sk first sl st, working in **back lps** (*see Stitch Guide*), sl st in each of next 3 sts, sc in each of next 3 sts, hdc in each of last 3 sts, turn.

Row 4: Working in back lps, ch 1, hdc in each of first 3 sts, sc in each of next 3 sts, sl st in last 3 sts, sl st in same st on rnd 1, turn.

Row 5: Sk first sl st, working in back lps, sl st in each of next 3 sts, sc in each of next 3 sts, hdc in each of last 3 sts, turn.

Row 6: Working in back lps, ch 1, hdc in each of first 3 sts, sc in each of next 3 sts, sl st in each of last 3 sts, sl st in next st on rnd 1, turn.

Row 7: Sk first sl st, working back lps, sl st in each of next 3 sts, sc in each of next 3 sts, hdc in each of last 3 sts, turn. Fasten off.

Row 8: Join first color in first st, ch 1, hdc in same st and each of next 2 sts, sc in each of next 3 sts, sl st in each of last 3 sts, sl st in next st on rnd 1, turn.

Row 9: Sk first sl st, working in back lps, sl st in each of next 3 sts, sc in each of next 3 sts, hdc in each of last 3 sts, turn. Fasten off.

Row 10: Join next color in first st, ch 1, hdc in same st and each of next 2 sts, sc in each of next 3 sts, sl st in each of last 3 sts, sl st in same st on rnd 1, turn.

Row 11: Sk first sl st, working in back lps, sl st in each of next 3 sts, sc in each of next 3 sts, hdc in each of last 3 sts, turn.

Row 12: Working in back lps, ch 1, hdc in each of first 3 sts, sc in each of next 3 sts, sl st in each of last 3 sts, sl st in next st on rnd 1, turn.

Row 13: Sk first sl st, working back lps, sl st in each of next 3 sts, sc in each of next 3 sts, hdc in each of last 3 sts, turn.

Row 14: Ch 1, hdc in same st and each of next 2 sts, sc in each of next 3 sts, sl st in each of last 3 sts, sl st in same st on rnd 1, turn.

Row 15: Sk first sl st, working back lps, sl st in each of next 3 sts, sc in each of next 3 sts, hdc in each of last 3 sts, turn. Fasten off.

Rows 16 & 17: Rep rows 8 & 9.

Rows 18–71: [Rep rows 10–17 consecutively] 9 times, ending last rep with row 15 alternating colors with 2 rows of first color between each color.

Row 72: Join first color in first st, hdc in same st and in each of next 2 sts, sc in each of next 3 sts, sl st in each of last 3 sts, sl st in same st as first st on rnd 1, turn.

Row 73: Rep row 9.

Working in back lps, sew rows 2 and 73 tog.

EDGING
Rnd 1: Now working in rnds and in ends of rows around outer edge, join first color with sc in end of any row, evenly sp 71 sc around, join in beg sc. (72 sc)

Rnd 2: Ch 4 (counts as first tr), (2 tr, ch 2, 3 tr) in same st (corner), *ch 1, sk next 3 sts, (2 dc, ch 1, 2 dc) in next st, ch 1, sk next 3 sts, 3 hdc in next st, ch 1, sk next st, 3 hdc in next st, ch 1, sk next 3 sts, (2 dc, ch 1, 2 dc) in next st, ch 1, sk next 3 sts**, (3 tr, ch 2, 3 tr) in next st (corner), rep from * around, ending last rep at **, join in 4th ch of beg ch-4.

Rnd 3: Ch 1, sc in each st and in each ch-1 sp around, with 3 sc in each corner ch-2 sp, join in beg sc. Fasten off. ■

Square 90

FINISHED SIZE
6 inches in diameter

GAUGE
Rnds 1 & 2 = 3 inches in diameter

PATTERN NOTES
Join with slip stitch as indicated unless otherwise stated.

Square is made with 1 color of medium (worsted) weight yarn.

INSTRUCTIONS
SQUARE

Rnd 1: With size H hook, ch 2, 8 sc in 2nd ch from hook, **join** (*see Pattern Notes*) in beg sc.

Rnd 2: Ch 1, sc in first st, *ch 4, sc in 2nd ch from hook, hdc in next ch, tr in last ch (*point*), sk next st on rnd 1**, sc in next st, rep from * around, ending last rep at **, join in beg sc.

Rnd 3: Ch 8 (*counts as first dc and ch-5*), *sc in tip of next point, ch 5**, dc in next sc between points, ch 5, rep between * around, ending last rep at **, join in 3rd ch of beg ch-8.

Rnd 4: Sl st in each of next 2 chs, ch 1, sc in same ch sp, ch 7, [sc in next ch sp, ch 7] around, join in beg sc.

Rnd 5: Sl st in first ch sp, ch 5 (*counts as first dtr*), (6 dtr, ch 3, 7 dtr) in same ch sp, *sc in next ch sp**, (7 dtr, ch 3, 7 dtr) in next ch sp, rep from * around, ending last rep at **, join in 5th ch of beg ch-5. Fasten off. ∎

Square 91

FINISHED SIZE
7 inches square

GAUGE
Rnds 1 & 2 = 3½ inches in diameter

PATTERN NOTES
Chain-3 at beginning of row or round counts as first double crochet unless otherwise stated.

Join with slip stitch as indicated unless otherwise stated.

Square is made with 1 color of medium (worsted) weight yarn.

INSTRUCTIONS
SQUARE

Rnd 1: With size H hook, ch 4, sl st in first ch to form ring, **ch 3** (*see Pattern Notes*), dc in ring, ch 3, [2 dc in ring, ch 3] 7 times, **join** (*see Pattern Notes*) 3rd ch of beg ch-3.

Rnd 2: Sl st in next st, sl st in next ch sp, ch 3, (dc, ch 2, 2 dc) in same ch sp (*corner*), *ch 3, sc in next ch sp, ch 3**, (2 dc, ch 3, 2 dc) in next ch sp (*corner*), rep from * around, ending last rep at **, join in 3rd ch of beg ch-3.

Rnd 3: Sl st in next st, sl st in next ch sp, ch 3, (dc, ch 3, 2 dc) in same ch sp, *[ch 3, sc in next ch sp] twice, ch 3**, (2 dc, ch 3, 2 dc) in next corner ch sp, rep from * around, ending last rep at **, join in 3rd ch of beg ch-3.

Rnd 4: Sl st in next st, sl st in next ch sp, ch 3, (dc, ch 3, 2 dc) in same ch sp, *ch 3, sk next ch sp, (dc, {ch 1, dc} 5 times) in next ch sp, ch 3, sk next ch sp**, (2 dc, ch 3, 2 dc) in next ch sp, rep from * around, ending last rep at **, join in 3rd ch of beg ch-3.

Rnd 5: Sl st in next st, sl st in next ch sp, ch 3, (dc, ch 2, 2 dc, ch 3, 2 dc, ch 2, 2 dc) in same ch sp, *ch 3, sk next 2 sts, sc in next st, [ch 3, sk next ch sp, sc in next st] 5 times, ch 3, sk next 2 sts**, (2 dc, ch 2, 2 dc, ch 3, 2 dc, ch 2, 2 dc) in next ch sp, rep from * around, ending last rep at **, join in 3rd ch of beg ch-3. Fasten off. ∎

Square 92

FINISHED SIZE
5½ inches square

GAUGE
Rnds 1 & 2 = 2½ inches in diameter

PATTERN NOTES
Chain-3 at beginning of row or round counts as first double crochet unless otherwise stated.

Join with slip stitch as indicated unless otherwise stated.

Square is made with 1 color of medium (worsted) weight yarn.

SPECIAL STITCHES
Beginning cluster (beg cl): Ch 3 (*counts as first dc*), holding back last lp of each st on hook, 4 dc in place indicated, yo, pull through all lps on hook.

Cluster (cl): Holding back last lp of each st on hook, 5 dc in place indicated, yo, pull through all lps on hook.

INSTRUCTIONS
SQUARE
Rnd 1: With size H hook, ch 4, sl st in first ch to form ring, ch 4 (*counts as first dc and ch-1*), [dc in ring, ch 1] 7 times, **join** (*see Pattern Notes*) in 3rd ch of beg ch-4.

Rnd 2: Sl st in first ch sp, ch 1, sc in same ch sp, ch 3, [sc in next ch sp, ch 3] around, join in beg sc.

Rnd 3: Sl st in next ch sp, ch 1, sc in same ch sp, ch 5, [sc in next ch sp, ch 5] around, join in beg sc.

Rnd 4: Sl st in first ch sp, ch 1, 7 sc in same ch sp and in each ch sp around, join in beg sc.

Rnd 5: Sl st in next st, **beg cl** (*see Special Stitches*) in same st,*[ch 5, sk next st, **cl** (*see Special Stitches*)] twice, ch 5, sc in center sc of next sc group, ch 5**, cl in 2nd sc of next sc group, rep from * around, ending last rep at **, join in beg cl.

Rnd 6: Sl st in each of next 2 chs of next ch-5 sp, ch 1, sc in same ch sp, *ch 7, [sc in next ch sp, ch 5] 3 times**, sc in next ch sp, rep from * around, ending last rep at **, join in beg sc. Fasten off. ∎

Square 93

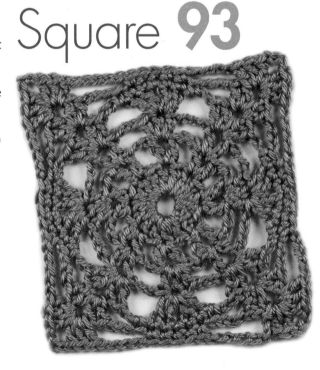

FINISHED SIZE
6 inches square

GAUGE
Rnds 1 & 2 = 3 inches in diameter

PATTERN NOTES
Chain-3 at beginning of row or round counts as first double crochet unless otherwise stated.

Join with slip stitch as indicated unless otherwise stated.

Square is made with 1 color of medium (worsted) weight yarn.

INSTRUCTIONS
SQUARE
Rnd 1: With size H hook, ch 4, sl st in first ch to form ring, **ch 3** (*see Pattern Notes*), 15 dc in ring, **join** (*see Pattern Notes*) 3rd ch of beg ch-3.

Rnd 2: Ch 4 (*counts as first dc and ch-1*), dc in same st, ch 2, sk next st, [(dc, ch 1, dc) in next st, ch 2, sk next st] around, join in 3rd ch of beg ch-4.

Rnd 3: Sl st in first ch-1 sp, ch 4, dc in same ch sp, *ch 3, sk next ch-2 sp, 3 dc in next ch-1 sp, ch 3, sk next ch-2 sp**, (dc, ch 1, dc) in next ch-1 sp, rep from * around, ending last rep at **, join in 3rd ch of beg ch-3.

Rnd 4: Sl st in first ch sp, ch 3, (dc, ch 2, 2 dc) in same ch sp, *ch 3, sk next ch sp, (2 dc, ch 3, 2 dc) in center st of next dc group, ch 3, sk next ch sp**, (2 dc, ch 2, 2 dc) in next ch sp, rep from * around, ending last rep at **, join in 3rd ch of beg ch-3.

Rnd 5: Sl st in next st, sl st in next ch sp, ch 3, (dc, ch 2, 2 dc) in same ch sp (*corner*), *ch 3, sc in next ch sp, sc in each of next 2 sts, sc in next ch sp, sc in each of next 2 sts, sc in next ch sp, ch 3**, (2 dc, ch 2, 2 dc) in next ch sp (*corner*), rep from * around, ending last rep at **, join in 3rd ch of beg ch-3.

Rnd 6: Sl st in next st, sl st in next ch sp, ch 3, (2 dc, ch 3, 3 dc) in same ch sp, *ch 5, sk next 3 sts, sc in each of next 5 sc, ch 5, sk next 3 sts**, (3 dc, ch 3, 3 dc) in next ch sp, rep from * around, ending last rep at **, join in 3rd ch of beg ch-3. Fasten off. ∎

Square 94

FINISHED SIZE
7 inches square

GAUGE
Rnds 1 & 2 = 2 inches in diameter

PATTERN NOTES
Chain-3 at beginning of row or round counts as first double crochet unless otherwise stated.

Join with slip stitch as indicated unless otherwise stated.

Square is made with 1 color of medium (worsted) weight yarn.

INSTRUCTIONS
SQUARE
Rnd 1: With size H hook, ch 6, sl st in first ch to form ring, ch 1, 8 sc in ring, **join** (*see Pattern Notes*) in beg sc. (*8 sc*)

Rnd 2: **Ch 3** *(see Pattern Notes)*, dc in same st, 2 dc in each st around, join in 3rd ch of beg ch-3. *(16 dc)*

Rnd 3: Ch 1, sc in first st, ch 10, sc in same st, *sc in next st, (sc, ch 4, sc) in next st, sc in next st**, (sc, ch 10, sc) in next st, rep from * around, ending last rep at **, join in beg sc.

Rnd 4: Sl st in first ch sp, ch 1, (sc, {ch 3, sc} 4 times) in same ch sp, *ch 2, dc in next ch sp, ch 2**, (sc, {ch 3, sc} 4 times) in next ch sp, rep from * around, ending last rep at **, join in beg sc.

Rnd 5: Sl st in first ch sp, ch 1, sc in same ch sp, *ch 3, (sc, ch 3, sc) in next ch sp, ch 3, sc in next ch sp, ch 3, sk next 2 ch sps, (sc, ch 3, sc) in next dc, ch 3, sk next ch sp**, sc in next ch sp, rep from * around, ending last rep at **, join in beg sc.

Rnd 6: Sl st in first ch sp, ch 1, sc in same ch sp, *ch 1, 3 sc in next ch sp, ch 3, sk next 2 ch sp, (2 tr, ch 3, 2 tr) in next ch sp *(corner)*, ch 3, sk next ch sp**, sc in next ch sp, rep from * around, ending last rep at **, join in beg sc.

Rnd 7: Sl st in next ch sp, sl st in next st, ch 1, *(sc, ch 2, sc) in next st, ch 3, sk next sc and next ch sp, dc in each of next 2 tr, (3 tr, ch 3, sl st in 3rd ch from hook, 3 tr) in next corner ch sp, dc in each of next 2 tr, ch 3, sk next 2 ch sps, rep from * around, join in beg sc. Fasten off. ∎

Square 95

FINISHED SIZE
6½ inches square

GAUGE
Rnds 1 & 2 = 3 inches in diameter

PATTERN NOTES
Chain-3 at beginning of row or round counts as first double crochet unless otherwise stated.

Join with slip stitch as indicated unless otherwise stated.

Square is made with 1 color of medium (worsted) weight yarn.

SPECIAL STITCHES
Beginning cluster (beg cl): Ch 3 *(counts as first dc)*, holding back last lp of each st on hook, 2 dc in place indicated, yo, pull through all lps on hook.

Cluster (cl): Holding back last lp of each st on hook, 3 dc in place indicated, yo, pull through all lps on hook.

INSTRUCTIONS
SQUARE

Rnd 1: With size H hook, ch 6, sl st in first ch to form ring, **ch 3** *(see Pattern Notes)*, 15 dc in ring, **join** *(see Pattern Notes)* 3rd ch of beg ch-3. *(16 dc)*

Rnd 2: Ch 5 *(counts as first dc and ch-2)*, [dc in next st, ch 2] around, join in 3rd ch of beg ch-5.

Rnd 3: Sl st in first ch sp, **beg cl** *(see Special Stitches)* in same ch sp, ch 2, [**cl** *(see Special Stitches)* in next ch sp, ch 2] around, join in beg cl.

Rnd 4: Sl st in first ch sp, ch 1, sc in same ch sp, ch 3, [sc in next ch sp, ch 3] around, join in beg sc.

Rnd 5: Sl st in first ch sp, ch 1, sc in same ch sp, ch 5, [sc in next ch sp, ch 5] around, join in beg sc.

Rnd 6: Sl st in first ch sp, (beg cl, ch 2, dc, ch 2, cl) in same ch sp *(corner)*, *ch 2, [sc in next ch sp, ch 3] twice, sc in next ch sp, ch 2**, (cl, ch 2, dc, ch 2, cl) in next ch sp *(corner)*, rep from * around, ending last rep at **, join in beg cl.

Rnd 7: Sl st in first ch sp, (beg cl, ch 2, cl) in same ch sp, *ch 2, cl in next ch sp, ch 3, (sc, ch 3, sc) in each of next 3 ch sps, ch 3, cl in next ch sp, ch 2**, (cl, ch 2, cl) in next ch sp, rep from * around, ending last rep at **, join in beg cl. Fasten off. ■

Square 96

FINISHED SIZE
5½ inches square

GAUGE
Rnds 1 & 2 = 1½ inches in diameter

PATTERN NOTES
Join with slip stitch as indicated unless otherwise stated.

Square is made with 3 colors of medium (worsted) weight yarn.

SPECIAL STITCH
Cluster (cl): Ch 5, holding back last lp of each st on hook, 3 dtr in same place, yo, pull through all lps on hook.

INSTRUCTIONS
SQUARE

Rnd 1: With size H hook, ch 4, 7 dc in 4th ch from hook *(first 3 chs count as first dc)*, **join** *(see Pattern Notes)* 3rd ch of beg ch-3. *(8 dc)*

Rnd 2: Ch 1, sc in each st around, join in beg sc. Fasten off.

Rnd 3: Join next color in any st, *cl *(see Special Stitch)* in same st, ch 5, sl st in same st *(petal)***, sl st in next st, rep from * around, ending last rep at **, join in beg sl st. Fasten off.

Rnd 4: Working behind petals, join next color with sc in sp between petals, ch 5, [sc in sp between next 2 petals, ch 5] around, join in beg sc.

Rnd 5: Sl st in first ch sp, ch 1, sc in same ch sp, ch 5, [sc in next ch sp, ch 5] around, join in beg sc.

Rnd 6: Sl st in each of first 2 chs of first ch sp, ch 1, sc in same ch sp, *ch 10, sc in next ch sp, ch 5**, sc in next ch sp, rep from * around, ending last rep at **, join in beg sc.

Rnd 7: Sl st in first ch sp, ch 3 *(counts as first dc)*, (4 dc, ch 5, 5 dc) in same ch sp, *5 dc in next ch sp**, (5 dc, ch 5, 5 dc) in next ch sp, rep from * around, ending last rep at **, join in 3rd ch of beg ch-3. Fasten off. ■

Square 97

FINISHED SIZE
4½ inches square

GAUGE
Rnds 1 & 2 = 3 inches in diameter

PATTERN NOTES
Chain-3 at beginning of row or round counts as first double crochet unless otherwise stated.

Join with slip stitch as indicated unless otherwise stated.

Square is made with 4 colors of medium (worsted) weight yarn.

SPECIAL STITCHES
Beginning cluster (beg cl): Ch 3 *(counts as first dc)*, holding back last lp of each st on hook, 3 dc in place indicated, yo, pull through all lps on hook.

Cluster (cl): Holding back last lp of each st on hook, 4 dc in place indicated, yo, pull through all lps on hook.

INSTRUCTIONS
SQUARE
Rnd 1: With size H hook, ch 4, sl st in first ch to form ring, ch 4 *(counts as first dc and ch-1)*, [dc in ring, ch 1] 7 times, **join** *(see Pattern Notes)* 3rd ch of beg ch-4. Fasten off.

Rnd 2: Join next color in any ch sp, **beg cl** *(see Special Stitches)* in same ch sp, ch 3, [**cl** *(see Special Stitches)* in next ch sp, ch 3] around, join in beg cl. Fasten off.

Rnd 3: Join next color in any ch sp, **ch 3** *(see Pattern Notes)*, (2 dc, ch 3, 3 dc) in same ch sp *(corner)*, *ch 5, sk next ch sp**, (3 dc, ch 3, 3 dc) in next ch sp *(corner)*, rep from * around, ending last rep at **, join in 3rd ch of beg ch-3. Fasten off.

Rnd 4: Join next color with sc in any corner ch sp, ch 3, sc in same corner ch sp, *ch 2, working over ch-5 sp on last rnd, 7 dc in sk ch-3 sp on rnd 2, ch 2**, (sc, ch 3, sc) in next corner ch sp, rep from * around, ending last rep at **, join in beg sc. Fasten off. ■

Square 98

FINISHED SIZE
5½ inches square

GAUGE
Rnds 1 & 2 = 3 inches in diameter

PATTERN NOTES
Join with slip stitch as indicated unless otherwise stated.

Square is made with 1 color of medium (worsted) weight yarn.

SPECIAL STITCHES
Beginning 2-double crochet cluster (beg 2-dc cl): Ch 2, holding back last lp of each st on hook, dc in place indicated, yo, pull through all lps on hook.

2-double crochet cluster (2-dc cl): Holding back last lp of each st on hook, 2 dc in place indicated, yo, pull through all lps on hook.

3-double crochet cluster (3-dc cl): Holding back last lp of each st on hook, 3 dc in place indicated, yo, pull through all lps on hook.

Treble crochet cluster (tr cl): Holding back last lp of each st on hook, 4 tr in place indicated, yo, pull through all lps on hook.

INSTRUCTIONS
SQUARE
Rnd 1: With size H hook, ch 4, sl st in first ch to form ring, **beg 2-dc cl** (*see Special Stitches*) in ring, ch 2, [**2-dc cl** (*see Special Stitches*) in ring, ch 2] 7 times, **join** (*see Pattern Notes*) in beg 2-dc cl.

Rnd 2: Ch 7, **3-dc cl** (*see Special Stitches*) in 4th ch from hook (*first 3 chs count as first dc*), [dc in next st, ch 4, 3-dc cl in 4th ch from hook] around, join in 3rd ch of beg ch-7.

Rnd 3: Ch 6 (*counts as first dc and ch-3*), **tr cl** (*see Special Stitches*) in next dc, (ch 3, tr cl) twice in same st (*corner*), ch 3, [dc in next dc, ch 3, (tr cl, ch 3) 3 times in next dc (*corner*)] around, join in 3rd ch of beg ch-6.

Rnd 4: Ch 2 (*counts as first hdc*), 3 hdc in each ch sp and hdc in each st around with (dc, ch 3,

hdc) in each center tr cl in corners, join in 2nd ch of beg ch-2. Fasten off. ∎

Square 99

FINISHED SIZE
3¾ inches square

GAUGE
Rnds 1 & 2 = 2 inches in diameter

PATTERN NOTES
Join with slip stitch as indicated unless otherwise stated.

Square is made with 3 colors of medium (worsted) weight yarn.

INSTRUCTIONS
SQUARE
Rnd 1 (RS): With size H hook, ch 2, 8 sc in 2nd ch from hook, **do not join.**

Rnd 2: Working in **front lps** (*see Stitch Guide*), sc in each st around, **join** (*see Pattern Notes*) in both lps of beg sc. Fasten off.

Rnd 3: Working in rem lps of rnd 1, join next color in any st, ch 3, dc in 3rd ch from hook, sl st in same st, *ch 2, sk next st**, (sl st, ch 3, dc in 3rd ch from hook, sl st) in next st, rep from * around, ending last rep at **, join in beg sl st. Fasten off.

Rnd 4: Join next color in any ch sp, ch 6 *(counts as first dc and ch-3)*, 3 dc in same ch sp, (3 dc, ch 3, 3 dc) in each ch sp around ending with 2 dc in same ch as first dc, join in 3rd ch of beg ch-6.

Rnd 5: Sl st in first ch sp, ch 3 *(counts as first dc)*, (dc, ch 3, 2 dc) in same ch sp, dc in each st around with (2 dc, ch 3, 2 dc) in each ch sp, join 3rd ch of beg ch-3. Fasten off. ■

Square 100

FINISHED SIZE
5½ inches square

GAUGE
Rnds 1 & 2 = 3 inches in diameter

PATTERN NOTES
Join with slip stitch as indicated unless otherwise stated.

Chain-3 at beginning of row or round count as first double crochet unless otherwise stated.

Square is made with 2 colors of medium (worsted) weight yarn.

SPECIAL STITCH
Picot: Ch 3, sl st in 3rd ch from hook.

INSTRUCTIONS
SQUARE
Rnd 1 (RS): With size H hook, ch 8, 3 tr in 4th ch from hook, tr in next ch, dc in next ch, hdc in next ch, 3 sc in last ch, working on opposite side of ch, hdc in next ch, dc in next ch, tr in next ch, (3 tr, ch 3, sl st) in same ch as first tr, **do not join.**

Rnd 2: Ch 1, sc in sl st just worked, ch 1, dc in ch-3, ch 1, 2 tr in next st, ch 1, 2 tr in next st, (dc, hdc) in next st, hdc in each of next 2 sts, sc in each of next 2 sts, 3 sc in next st, sc in each of next 2 sts, hdc in each of next 2 sts, (hdc, dc) in next st, 2 tr in next st, ch 1, 2 tr in next st, ch 1, dc in ch-3, ch 1, **join** *(see Pattern Notes)* in beg sc, **turn.**

Rnd 3: Ch 1, sc in first st, **picot** *(see Special Stitch)*, [sc in next st, picot] around, join in beg sl st. turn. Fasten off.

Rnd 4: Join next color in first st, ch 6 *(counts as first dc and ch-3)*, dc in same st, ch 1, [**fpsc** *(see Stitch Guide)* around next sc, ch 1] 5 times, fpsc around next sc, ch 4, [fpsc around next sc, ch 1] 5 times, fpsc around next sc, ch 4, sk next sc, [fpsc around next sc, ch 1] 5 times, fpsc around next sc, ch 4, [fpsc around next picot, ch 1] 6 times, join in 3rd ch of beg ch-6.

Rnd 5: Sl st in first ch sp, **ch 3** *(see Pattern Notes)*, (2 dc, ch 3, 3 dc) in same ch sp, ch 3, sk next 2 ch sps, sc in next ch sp, ch 3, sk next ch sp, sc in next ch sp, ch 3, sk next ch sp, (3 dc, ch 3, 3 dc) in next ch-4 sp, *[ch 3, sk next ch sp, sc in next ch sp] twice, ch 3, sk next ch sp, (3 dc, ch 3, 3 dc) in next ch-4 sp, rep from * twice, [ch 3, sk next ch sp, sc in next ch sp] twice, ch 3, sk last 2 ch sps, join in 3rd ch of beg ch-3.

Rnd 6: Sl st in each of next 2 sts, sl st in next ch sp, ch 3, (2 dc, ch 3, 3 dc) in same ch sp, *3 dc in next ch sp, working over ch sp on last rnd, 3 dc in sk ch sp on rnd 4, 3 dc in next ch sp on this rnd**, (3 dc, ch 3, 3 dc) in next ch sp, rep from * around, ending last rep at **, join in 3rd ch of beg ch-3. Fasten off. ■

Square 101

FINISHED SIZE
5½ inches square

GAUGE
Rnd 1 = 1½ inches in diameter

PATTERN NOTES
Chain-3 at beginning of row or round counts as first double crochet unless otherwise stated.

Join with slip stitch as indicated unless otherwise stated.

Square is made with 3 colors of medium (worsted) weight yarn.

INSTRUCTIONS
SQUARE
Rnd 1: With size H hook, ch 4, sl st in first ch to form ring, **ch 3** (*see Pattern Notes*), 11 dc in ring, **join** (*see Pattern Notes*) in 3rd ch of beg ch-3. Fasten off.

Rnd 2: Working in **front lps** (*see Stitch Guide*), join next color in first st, *ch 5, sc in 2nd ch from hook, dc in each of next 2 chs, sc in last ch (*petal*)**, sl st in next st, rep from * around, ending last rep at **, join in beg sl st. Fasten off.

Rnd 3: Working in **back lps** (*see Stitch Guide*) of rnd 1 in back of petals, join next color in any st, ch 3, dc in same st, 2 dc in each st around, join in 3rd ch of beg ch-3.

Rnd 4: Ch 1, sc in first st, ch 2, sk next st, [sc in next st, ch 2, sk next st] around, join in beg sc.

Rnd 5: Sl st in first ch sp, ch 3, (2 dc, ch 3, 3 dc) in same ch sp, *[ch 1, 3 dc in next ch sp] twice**, ch 1, (3 dc, ch 3, 3 dc) in next ch sp, rep from * around, ending last rep at **, join with sc in 3rd ch of beg ch-3 forming last ch sp.

Rnd 6: Ch 1, sc in this ch sp, *ch 3, (sc, ch 3, sc) in next ch sp**, [ch 3, sc in next ch sp] 3 times, rep from * around, ending last rep at **, ch 3, [sc in next ch sp, ch 3] around, join in beg sc. Fasten off.

Rnd 7: Join 2nd color with sc in any ch sp, 2 sc in same ch sp, ch 1, [3 sc in next ch sp, ch 1] around, join in beg sc. Fasten off. ∎

Annie's Attic®

TOLL-FREE ORDER LINE or to request a free catalog (800) LV-ANNIE (800) 582-6643
Customer Service (800) AT-ANNIE (800) 282-6643, **Fax** (800) 882-6643
Visit anniesattic.com

We have made every effort to ensure the accuracy and completeness of these instructions.
We cannot, however, be responsible for human error, typographical mistakes or variations in individual work.

ISBN: 978-1-59635-210-0
Library of Congress Control Number: 2008924593

Stitch Guide

For more complete information, visit **FreePatterns.com**

ABBREVIATIONS

beg	begin/beginning
bpdc	back post double crochet
bpsc	back post single crochet
bptr	back post treble crochet
CC	contrasting color
ch	chain stitch
ch--	refers to chain or space previously made (i.e., ch-1 space)
ch sp	chain space
cl	cluster
cm	centimeter(s)
dc	double crochet
dec	decrease/decreases/decreasing
dtr	double treble crochet
fpdc	front post double crochet
fpsc	front post single crochet
fptr	front post treble crochet
g	gram(s)
hdc	half double crochet
inc	increase/increases/increasing
lng	long
lp(s)	loop(s)
MC	main color
mm	millimeter(s)
oz	ounce(s)
pc	popcorn
rem	remain/remaining
rep	repeat(s)
rnd(s)	round(s)
RS	right side
sc	single crochet
sk	skip(ped)
sl st	slip stitch
sp(s)	space(s)
st(s)	stitch(es)
tog	together
tr	treble crochet
trtr	triple treble crochet
WS	wrong side
yd(s)	yard(s)
yo	yarn over

Chain—ch: Yo, pull through lp on hook.

Slip stitch—sl st: Insert hook in st, pull through both lps on hook.

Single crochet—sc: Insert hook in st, yo, pull through st, yo, pull through both lps on hook.

Front post stitch—fp: Back post stitch—bp: When working post st, insert hook from right to left around post st on previous row.

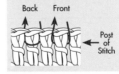

Back   Front

← Post of Stitch

Front loop—front lp Back loop— back lp

Front Loop   Back Loop

Half double crochet—hdc: Yo, insert hook in st, yo, pull through st, yo, pull through all 3 lps on hook.

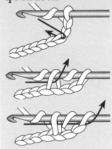

Double crochet—dc: Yo, insert hook in st, yo, pull through st, [yo, pull through 2 lps] twice.

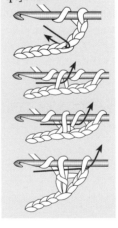

Change colors: Drop first color; with 2nd color, pull through last 2 lps of st.

Treble crochet—tr: Yo twice, insert hook in st, yo, pull through st, [yo, pull through 2 lps] 3 times.

Double treble crochet—dtr: Yo 3 times, insert hook in st, yo, pull through st, [yo, pull through 2 lps], 4 times.

Single crochet decrease (sc dec): (Insert hook, yo, draw lp through) in each of the sts indicated, yo, draw through all lps on hook.

Example of 2-sc dec

Half double crochet decrease (hdc dec): (Yo, insert hook, yo, draw lp through) in each of the sts indicated, yo, draw through all lps on hook.

Example of 2-hdc dec

Double crochet decrease (dc dec): (Yo, insert hook, yo, draw loop through, draw through 2 lps on hook) in each of the sts indicated, yo, draw through all lps on hook.

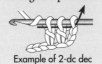

Example of 2-dc dec

Example of 2-tr dec

Treble crochet decrease (tr dec): Holding back last lp of each st, tr in each of the sts indicated, yo, pull through all lps on hook.

US		UK
sl st (slip stitch)	=	sc (single crochet)
sc (single crochet)	=	dc (double crochet)
hdc (half double crochet)	=	htr (half treble crochet)
dc (double crochet)	=	tr (treble crochet)
tr (treble crochet)	=	dtr (double treble crochet)
dtr (double treble crochet)	=	ttr (triple treble crochet)
skip	=	miss